Published in 1998 by
Aslib, The Association for Information Management
Staple Hall, Stone House Court, London EC3A 7PB

***

British Library Cataloguing in Publication Data
A catalogue record for this book is available from the British Library
ISBN 0 85142 414 7

Aslib, The Association for Information Management, is a world class corporate membership organization with over 2000 members in some 70 countries. Aslib actively promotes best practice in the management of information resources. It lobbies on all aspects of the management of and legislation concerning information at local, national and international levels.

Aslib provides consultancy and information services, professional development training, conferences, specialist recruitment, Internet products, and publishes primary and secondary journals, conference proceedings, directories and monographs.

Further information about Aslib can be obtained from:
Aslib, The Association for Information Management
Staple Hall, Stone House Court, London EC3A 7PB
Tel: +44 (0) 171 903 0000, Fax: +44 (0) 171 903 0011
Email pubs@aslib.co.uk, WWW http://www.aslib.co.uk/

Series Editor - Sylvia P. Webb

Sylvia Webb is a well known consultant, author and lecturer in the information management field. Her first book, *Creating an Information Service,* now in its third edition, was published by Aslib and has sold in over forty countries. She has experience of working in both the public and private sectors, ranging from public libraries to national and international organisations. She has also been a lecturer at Ashridge Management College, specialising in management and inter-personal skills, which led to her second book, *Personal Development in Information Work,* also published by Aslib. She has served on a number of government advisory bodies and is past Chair of the Information and Library Services Lead Body which develops National Vocational Qualifications (NVQs) for the LIS profession. She is actively involved in professional education with Aslib and the Library Association and is also a former Vice-President of the Institute of Information Scientists. As well as being editor of this series, Sylvia Webb has written three of the Know How Guides: *Making a charge for library and information services, Preparing a guide to your library and information service* and *Knowledge management: linch-pin of change.*

A list of titles in the Aslib Know How Series appears on the back cover of this volume.

KNOWLEDGE MANAGEMENT:
linchpin of change

Some practical guidelines

Sylvia P Webb

The Aslib Know How Series

Editor: Sylvia P Webb

 **THE ASSOCIATION FOR INFORMATION MANAGEMENT**

Acknowledgements

I would like to thank the following individuals for their time and various contributions, which are much appreciated: Chris Cooper, Elizabeth Lank, Susan Moore, Barbara Salmon, Gwenda Sippings, David Skyrme, Sandra Ward, Stuart Ward, David Wilson, and especially the following organisations for their willingness to share their experience of knowledge management: Clifford Chance, ICL, PricewaterhouseCoopers.

Contents

1. SETTING THE SCENE   **1**

Introduction 1

What is knowledge management? 1

The processing hierarchy 3

2. KEY MANAGEMENT CONSIDERATIONS AND INFLUENCES   **7**

Managing change: the corporate culture 8

Changes in working practices 9

Formalising knowledge sharing 10

Consultation and communication 10

Questions for management 11

The Board Agenda - 10 key questions: 11

Tests for knowledge management 12

Defining knowledge management 13

Further questions and issues to be addressed 14

3. GETTING STARTED: INITIAL TASKS   **17**

Shaping the policy 17

Consultation mechanisms 18

The knowledge audit 21

Key points regarding the knowledge audit 22

4. NEXT STEPS   **24**

5. DAY-TO-DAY OPERATION: MANAGEMENT AND RELATED SKILLS

    27

Key tasks and responsibility 27

Keeping up to date 29

Summary of required skills and competencies 30

General day-to-day operational skills 31

Knowledge & information management skills 31

6. SYSTEMS AND SOFTWARE   **33**

7. MEASURING THE VALUE OF KNOWLEDGE   **35**
The use of non-financial measures 36

8. CONCLUSIONS   **38**

9. CASE STUDIES   **40**
1 - The PricewaterhouseCoopers Information and Knowledge Exchange (IKE) **40**
The Information and Knowledge Exchange (IKE) 41
The knowledge hubs 42
Organisation of the knowledge hubs 43
Key requirements of the knowledge hub role 44
Previous careers of knowledge hub specialists 48
Adopting the knowledge hub role 48
The Hub Manager Competency Framework 49
Hub manager training 52
2 - Valuing ICL knowledge **54**
Background *54*
Building the business case 54
Deciding where to start *55*
Developing Café VIK 56
The road show *56*
Sustaining a knowledge-sharing environment 57
Some lessons learned 59
Conclusions 59
3: Management of know-how in an international City law firm **60**
Use of intranets 61
Contribution and collection of know-how 62

References and further reading   **64**

Appendix: Useful organisations and contacts   **67**

1. SETTING THE SCENE

Introduction

There are many excellent books which discuss the concept of knowledge management in detail. The aim of this publication is to provide some practical guidelines for those interested in, or likely to be involved in, the implementation process and the subsequent knowledge management operation, whatever their current role. Some discussion of the subject does take place to put it into context; definitions are given and references made to key works in the field, along with suggestions of additional sources to consult. Questions to be addressed and issues to be considered are put forward. Case studies have been produced to illustrate different aspects of implementation and operation. Contact details of organisations and individuals who might assist further are also listed. It is hoped that this approach will provide a helpful starting point for those taking part in the development of a knowledge management function.

What is knowledge management?

Two of the most frequently asked questions about the subject of knowledge management seem to be "What exactly is it?" or alternatively "Is it a new name for information management?" Information is not a synonym for knowledge, which is an intellectual concept, referring to the condition of knowing or understanding something. Bonaventura (1997) suggests that neither data nor information on their own should be regarded as knowledge. He says that "Rather information is the potential for knowledge" noting that information will have to be worked upon, developed and applied; thus "Knowledge then, can be considered as output(s) from a continuous feedback loop which refines information through the application of that information."

In a discussion about information and knowledge Badenoch et al.(1994) note the difficulty of defining knowledge, saying that "many different disciplines use the term to denote different things". They see knowledge as being "personal, individual and inaccessible" which could make it difficult to harness; but they go on to say that "it does, however, manifest itself in (and is created and modified by) information". They also describe knowledge as a "dynamic, self-modifying state" which "changes in the course of acquiring information". This demonstrates the

1

close relationship between the two concepts and why the terms which describe them are sometimes used interchangeably. In seeking definitions of both knowledge and information Badenoch and his colleagues consulted key sources in the field and found what could be the simplest definition of all: that knowledge is "organised information in people's heads", Stonier (1990).

Various terms are used to describe what are seen as different types of knowledge. The two most commonly referred to in the business context are "explicit" and "tacit" knowledge. According to Nonaka & Takeuchi (1995) explicit knowledge can be articulated in formal language and transmitted through, for example, manuals, written specifications etc. Tacit knowledge is seen as personal knowledge, based on individual experience and values and therefore not as easily transmitted. However once the sharing of tacit knowledge has become part of the corporate culture, and it has been harnessed accordingly it will not be lost to the organisation if a particular individual moves on. By then it will have become embedded in the organisation as noted by Badaracco (1991). A practical example of the way in which knowledge might not only become embedded in a single organisation, but also have the potential to be organised to be accessible more widely is decribed by Vernon (1998). This case study looks at an initiative in cancer nursing education in the UK, in which knowledge has been organised in such a way as to enable others to share and acquire it. This is the development of a package in CD-ROM format with the prototype running as a help-file database allowing users to navigate its content via hypertext links. The multimedia nature of the product allows users to learn, for example, by seeing procedures demonstrated, or having a dynamic illustration as an explanation of the way in which certain drugs work. This demonstrates the potential of combining individual expert knowledge with technology to allow widespread flexible access and encourage further learning according to need.

Information and knowledge can be seen as closely related and complementary stages along the same road, and as such both perform essential roles in the decision-making process. Wilson (1996) presents a useful illustration of this with the notion of the processing hierarchy. This shows that by selecting and analysing data, information can be produced; by selecting and combining information, knowledge can be generated; from this decisions can be made and action taken. Wilson has produced a simple yet extremely helpful diagram setting out the inter-relationships of the different concepts, with a short textual example which puts it into an everyday context.

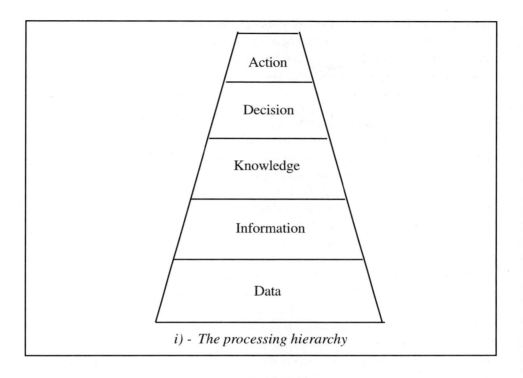

i) - The processing hierarchy

"For instance if you are standing on the platform at Paddington Station wanting to go to Oxford, you may consult a timetable (data) to look up the departure time of the next train (information). Then you may look at your watch to see what time it is (more information) and substract this from the departure time so that you know how long you have to wait (knowledge). Along with knowledge of the other options open to you, you can then decide what there is time for: enough only to board the train?...or to buy a newspaper first?...or to sit down with newspaper, coffee and bun? (decision and action)."

ii) - Textual example

Both the above are reproduced from Wilson, D.A. Managing knowledge. Oxford: Butterworth-Heinemann in conjunction with the Institute of Management, 1996, by kind permission of the author and publisher.

Disagreement over the meaning of the word "knowledge" is certainly not new, as Nonaka & Takeuchi (1995) demonstrate in their helpful introduction to the theory of the subject with its philosophical roots in earlier civilisations. However the notion of its formal management as an asset is more recent.

My own interest in what is currently referred to as knowledge management started some years ago. It came about in part through consideration of the way in which human beings think and operate in the work situation and arose out of earlier study in social psychology, and later through noting and monitoring the appearance and use of the term "know-how" in the business press. Although as already indicated, the concept of knowledge itself had been discussed and written about over a very long period of time, the issue of knowledge management had at that time, in the 1980s, not been widely documented in terms of its role in business strategy and management applications and the related impact on information provision and use within organisations. There were notable exceptions such as the early work of Sveiby and Lloyd (1987), and Noneka (1989), which drew attention to the formerly neglected corporate asset, namely its intellectual wealth. Although it is often suggested that what is today referred to as knowledge management was actually taking place in one form or another, there was a lack of openness about such activities, perhaps seen as giving away competitive advantage. Also, there seems to have been no widespread awareness of its potential. This therefore represented an exciting development with considerable implications for the future direction and success of a range of organisations and one which today is receiving far greater attention - you have only to look at the business press or visit any business bookshop. As for Websites, just enter the term "knowledge management" and you will be overwhelmed by the number of sites which claim to cover the subject. At the time of writing I have done just that and got the response that there are currently 137038 of these. By the time you read this there will probably be many more. (Of course you could refine the search term, or save time by noting any evaluations or descriptions of sites which are have been tried and tested, as regularly featured in the journal *Knowledge Management*; (see also Appendix).

Knowledge and individual expertise, as well as information, are now seen as vital to the success of a business. This is clearly demonstrated in the case studies which have been prepared for this publication. Strong evidence of the benefits of formally harnessing such assets is also set out in the report of a study of the development and impact of know-how databases (in effect knowledge management functions) in legal firms, Webb (1996).

Knowledge management is not only a key function of the commercial world; it is also relevant and applicable to many other types of organisation, as is reflected in the range of services described in the brochures of management consultancy firms and in the sessions presented at numerous knowledge management conferences. There are also now specialist journals devoted to the topic. The articles in these suggest varying views on what knowledge management is, ranging from "a new management fad?" to "something we have been doing for years but without giving it a name". This latter point also suggests that it has not been systematically pursued as a formal management activity, and that without such an approach its potential may not have been fully realised.

There seems to be agreement across various types of organisation that knowledge management contains a combination of some or all of the following features:

- recognising and building on in-house individual expertise
- formalising to varying degrees the harnessing of knowledge through the use of appropriate systems
- passing on knowledge
- developing it from an individual asset into a corporate one
- encouraging the growth of an open corporate culture in which knowledge is viewed as being central to organisational development and to the efficiency of methods of business operation.

Technology is seen to play a central role in the process, providing a sophisticated facility by which to store, organise and index details of wide-ranging expertise for future retrieval and ultimate contribution to the corporate good.

As with all good management practices, the climate in which knowledge management is able to operate effectively will need to be created through clear statements from top management and the use of appropriate communication mechanisms to ensure widespread understanding of, and commitment to both its aims and its operation. This will require careful planning of relevant staff development and training programmes, as well as the use of appropriate systems and procedures, and continuous monitoring of these to ensure that they remain effective. As Broadbent (1998) points out "Managing knowledge goes much further than capturing data and manipulating it to obtain information." The attributes of all those involved in the process provide the key to its success. Hamel (1995) notes that "A company's value derives not from things, but from knowledge, know-how, intellectual assets, competencies - all embodied in people." Rosenzweig (1998) in discussing strategies for global business, says that "A diverse workforce includes people with different world views and experiences. Making the most of diversity means forging a work environment that facilitates the sharing of ideas and the exchange of insights, inspiring novel solutions to problems." So there is increasing realisation of the importance of top management being aware of the potential of the individual as a key contributor to company strategy through knowledge management.

As this short introduction will have indicated already, there are a number of factors which an organisation will have to consider and act upon if it is to make the most of the knowledge and expertise which is present within it or is otherwise accessible. This guide sets out the key considerations and provides some practical guidelines to assist in developing and operating an effective knowledge management function. The way in which organisations operating in different sectors have gone about putting knowledge management into practice, is described in the three case studies in Chapter 9.

2. KEY MANAGEMENT CONSIDERATIONS AND INFLUENCES

Knowledge management, as with any organisational development or activity, is likely to be considered from the viewpoint of what it can contribute to organisational success, given the corporate aims and objectives. These in turn may suggest different ways of operating, but all organisations can benefit from having access to and making use of knowledge and information. The better it is managed, the more they are likely to benefit from it.

As pointed out by Quelin (1998), Associate Professor at the HEC School of Management in Paris, the acquisition of new knowledge and competencies is becoming more important as global competition accelerates. He also suggests that inter-company co-operation may be the way forward. Whilst this could be an anathema to some who might see it as threatening their own competitive advantage, Quelin notes that long experience of co-operating in research and development (R & D) across companies has presented opportunities for learning and the transfer of knowledge. However he also notes the possible hurdles to be overcome and the need to create an appropriate climate in which such developments can take place.

The mutual benefits of cooperation, not only between different organisations but also across sectors, are described in two recent cases of the sharing of knowledge and expertise among space agencies and the medical world, Eadie (1998). The first concerns space cool-suits and their potential for use by multiple sclerosis patients - work carried out by NASA with the Multiple Sclerosis Association of America; the second refers to the European Space Agency's work with certain metals, Shape Memory Alloys, and their subsequent application in dentistry and orthopaedic work.

The increasingly global nature of business also means that subsidiaries in every country of operation will need to accumulate their own local knowledge. Govindarajan & Gupta (1998) see some of this knowledge as being relevant across several countries and bringing a number of benefits if developed effectively. These include faster product and process innovation with lower costs, and a reduced risk of competitive pre-emption.

Roos (1998), who has done considerable work in the field of intellectual capital and effective strategy processes, considers the implications for managers of operating in a global economy in which knowledge is the prime source of competitive advantage. He notes particularly the importance of knowledge sharing through organised networks, but also warns of the need for sensitivity in dealing with those involved in the process, suggesting that problems could arise if people are treated merely as assets that can churn out knowledge on demand.

The above discussion shows the nature of the changes which are taking place and the way in which knowledge is central to the process.

Managing change: the corporate culture

In the current climate of rapid change, whether political, economic, social or technological, the introduction of any new management approach or technique, including knowledge management, may meet resistance or may be seen to fail for various reasons. For example, it is suggested by Ward (1998) that there are organisations which think they are ready to implement a knowledge management strategy, but are not exhibiting the appropriate corporate behaviour, largely because they misunderstand the key requirements and characteristics of a knowledge-focussed organisation.

The corporate culture then is likely to be the first candidate for change in today's organisation if knowledge management is to be effective. This may already be changing for other reasons, but the major change required with regard to knowledge management is one of openness with an emphasis on the systematic sharing and exchange of knowledge. This could represent a radical shift in some organisations where, as already indicated, the climate may be one where the tendency is for individuals to keep valuable knowledge to themselves to use when they see fit for personal career gain. This is illustrated by the results of research carried out by Skyrme & Amidon (1997) which showed that "the greatest inhibitor to knowledge sharing was inappropriate behaviours and organisational culture. The syndrome 'knowledge is power' predominates too often".

There is another reason for any new development being regarded with suspicion or at least caution by some employees. Organisations and the people working within them may feel less secure than in previous times, particularly given the current climate of change of ownership, through flotations and an increasing number of mergers and acquisitions. These may well involve restructuring and relocation, with job security, rather than knowledge sharing, likely to be uppermost in the minds of employees. Bonaventura (1997) suggests that "when jobs are at stake, networks are withdrawn and individual knowledge is closely guarded as protection against termination".

In such a climate any kind of change will have to be promoted to staff as part of overall policy and strategy for future success and survival. The management of change involves not only taking account of new legal and financial requirements or the changing, and increasingly competitive economic climate, but also of noting other changes which will influence the way in which the organisation operates. As well as keeping up-to-date with changes in its own markets and areas of activity, there will be other developments which apply across the board, regardless of sector or function. Some of these have a special relevance to the management of knowledge.

Changes in working practices
The impact of new technology on all aspects of operation has been widely acknowledged, but equally crucial to success is the implementation of various changes in working practices. These can have a considerable influence on the way in which operations are managed and services delivered.

Team working is seen to be a valuable contributor to the success of a knowledge-centred organisation. If team working is to be effective, it will require balanced levels of experience and knowledge across the team, as well as efficient rota management if consistency of output is to be ensured. This is especially important where the service concerned is one of providing information or directing people to the appropriate knowledge expert.

Successful team working is itself dependent on the sharing of knowledge and will require appropriate procedures to be in place to facilitate this. It will also be influenced by other related developments such as changes in working hours and patterns of work, increased job sharing, and of course technology-based systems.

Outsourcing - the contracting out of certain services - is another working practice which has strong implications for the knowledge management function, given that function's certain dependence on information technology (IT). Along with telecommunications-based public enquiry services of all kinds, IT is seemingly a prime target for outsourcing. As IT outsourcing can cover support services as well as implementation, it is something which will have to receive early consideration in the planning of any knowledge management function.

Formalising knowledge sharing

The other part of the equation - the use of the word "systematic" - could also signal change in organisations where previously any exchange of information has been on an informal basis and usually based on conversation rather than on paper or via an electronic medium. This informal approach was common practice, as discovered during background research for a survey of know-how and information provision in legal firms, carried out by the author, Webb (1996). The ICL case study which appears in Chapter 9 shows this to have been the situation which led to an appreciation of the value of intellectual assets and of the need to treat these more systematically. The Knowledge Management Network at ICL started with the realisation "that a great deal of knowledge management happened already" but that it was "entirely uncoordinated".

So although knowledge has always been present in organisations, and to some extent shared, this has been very much on an *ad hoc* basis, particularly in the Western world, where until fairly recently it was certainly not overtly managed or promoted as the key to organisational success. This is in stark contrast to the situation in Japan, judging from the examples provided by Nonaka & Takeuchi (1995). In one of their case studies concerning the Kao organisation, they note the view of the chief executive, Yoshio Maruta, that "since creative ideas result from interaction, information sharing becomes the fundamental basis of management". Contrast this with the view expressed in a British survey by the Institute of Management, according to which 78% of the 3000 managers who took part saw failure to capture [and presumably therefore to be able to share] knowledge systematically as one of the most significant barriers to creating and retaining intellectual capital, Allday (1997).

Consultation and communication

So how can an organisation set about achieving the necessary shift? The first step is to create a climate conducive to such a development - as with many "first steps" this is often the most difficult one. It has already been demonstrated that changing the corporate culture is not something which can be achieved overnight. It requires careful consideration, particularly because of the importance of the human element to its success. One of the conclusions of the Institute of Management report mentioned in the previous paragraph is that "Having an open and participative culture which values the skills and contributions of employees at all levels is crucial to the effective management of intellectual capital".

The ICL case underlines the need not only for communication, but also for involvement which can supply valuable feedback for future direction. One-way communication about any proposed change is not enough. Early involvement of

10

all those who make up the organisation is essential. First they need information about what is proposed, and why. Benefits need to be stressed. People always want to know how new developments will affect them, both in terms of their daily responsibilities and their longer-term security. They may worry about the need to acquire additional skills, or having to do things differently. Reassurance and an understanding that their contribution is valued and needed has to be communicated. They also need to know that the new development has the full commitment of top management, both in terms of involvement and support. The benefits of this kind of active support are noted in the Clifford Chance case study in Chapter 9.

Questions for management

At this early stage there will be a number of key issues to be addressed by management. Some of these will be very similar to those raised through the IMPACT programme which looks at information as an organisational asset. As part of the IMPACT work the Hawley Committee (1995) produced a set of guidelines for consideration by companies in reviewing their use of information.

The Board Agenda - 10 key questions:

- **For the Board**

- Is all necessary and sufficient information used by the Board?

- Is the Board aware of the information aspects of all items on its agenda?

- Does its use of information comply with all external laws and regulations?

- **For Management**

- Are information assets classified by value and importance?

- Is all information necessary, sufficient, reliable, timely and consistent?

- Is there proper use of information in accordance with external standards?

- Are people capable and trained to safeguard and enhance information?

- Is there protection of information from theft, loss, misuse?

- Is information harnessed for maximum benefit of the organisation?

- Is there a strategy for information systems and implementation?

Reproduced from Information as an asset: the board agenda. A consultative report. + Checklist and explanatory notes. London: IMPACT PROGRAMME, with their kind permission (contact details in Appendix).

Very similar questions to those above could usefully be asked of companies when seeking to establish their approach to knowledge as a business asset.

Sandra Ward, Director of UK Information Services at Glaxo Wellcome R & D, and 1998 President of the Institute of Information Scientists, also suggests some questions which could form a useful basis from which to assess whether the climate exists in which a company is able to pursue knowledge management. These are listed below:

Tests for knowledge management

- Can we transfer knowledge easily to new employees?

- Is ours an information/knowledge sharing culture?

- Do we know what and where our knowledge assets are?

- Is knowledge organised and easy to find?

- Do we capture and share best practice?

- Do we learn from mistakes?

- Do we reward knowledge-sharing?

- Are we exploiting knowledge effectively and strategically?

- Does our knowledge walk out of the door as staff leave?

Reproduced from a presentation by Dr Sandra Ward, Glaxo Wellcome R & D with her kind permission

Another useful self-assessment checklist has been produced by Rajan et al. (1998) to assist organisations in auditing current practice in knowledge creation and exchange. This concentrates on three areas: systems, values and behaviours, and appears in a survey of good practice in organisations throughout Europe and elsewhere.

By seeking answers to all the above suggested sets of questions, corporate strengths on which to build will be identified, as will issues which will need further consideration and appropriate action.

Defining knowledge management

Questions relating to strategy and policy must be asked, but in order to do so there must first be within the organisation an agreed definition of knowledge management and what it is to include or exclude. This may vary from organisation to organisation. Reference has already been made to the differences in perception of what knowledge itself is, so is there any single precise definition of the term "knowledge management"? Perhaps not, or at least not one that would be appropriate to all organisational settings, given the variance in activity and culture and the degree of dependence on knowledge as opposed to what might be seen as being purely information.

Those organisations which are today increasingly being referred to as "people businesses" and which were earlier described by Sveiby & Lloyd (1987) as "know-how companies" - those heavily reliant upon the knowledge and expertise of their professionals - look to have been at the forefront in terms of reshaping policy to focus on knowledge management. Sveiby & Lloyd give as examples of know-how businesses, firms such as advertising agencies, computer consultants, lawyers and management consultants. The case studies in Chapter 9 reinforce this choice of examples of businesses whose role it is to provide solutions. They include statements such as "The knowledge and skills of our consultants are our only enduring asset" (PricewaterhouseCoopers); "Experience and knowledge is vital to the work of successful lawyers" (Clifford Chance); "The company has been transforming itself into a service-led organisation whose knowledge **about** technology is its real asset. This transformation has made it a strategic imperative for ICL to excel at leveraging its intellectual capital across the world" (ICL).

Returning to the subject of definition, one of the lessons learned at ICL was that "significant time can be wasted debating the difference between information management and knowledge management" and that in their view "it is helpful to think of knowledge as something that comes from an interaction between people - and to view information as raw material for knowledge".

The definition of "know-how" drawn up specifically for use in the study of legal firms, Webb (1996), might be helpful as an example. Obviously the focus would change in a different setting, but the approach would be very similar. It is as follows:

"**Know-How** is a combination of the personal knowledge and experience of individuals, formerly disseminated largely through personal exchanges among lawyers. Know-how databases include detailed accounts of practical expertise present within the firm such as facts, rulings and opinions based on individual legal knowledge and experience. It assists in illustrating the ways in which rules have been applied and in informing the consideration of new cases. It is now increasingly being recorded in electronic form and collated into sophisticated databases, having been analysed in detail and indexed for precise retrieval. Indexing may be carried out by legal professionals who are seen to make their own know-how input, adding value to the process and to subsequent retrieval. It may also be part of the function of the firm's library and information service (LIS). Know-how may be organised for wide access through a firm's international or national computer network, or for direct access by specific practice groups, who could draw on each other's databases according to the requirements of particular client assignments."

The study itself revealed the usefulness of being able to link these databases of personal expertise and related internal records, to published information such as statutes and textbooks. This enabled access to a comprehensive range of material for anyone in the firm who needed to work on any particular aspect of law. This approach could similarly be applied, for example, in any research or project-based organisation or department dependent on specialist knowledge.

The important thing at this stage is that whatever the final wording of any definition, it must be capable of being accepted as both workable and relevant in terms of each organisation's specific responsibilities and objectives. Skyrme & Amidon (1997) provide a useful synthesis of some of the main definitions currently on offer. It is concise, incorporates the key elements of the process and could be used by most organisations as a starting point. Skyrme says: "Knowledge Management is the explicit and systematic management of vital knowledge and its associated processes of creation, organisation, diffusion, use and exploitation."

Further questions and issues to be addressed

Having agreed what it is, there will now be a need to address a range of fundamental questions such as:

- Where does knowledge management fit into the organisation's overall medium and long-term strategy?

- What identifiable benefits could it bring in terms of achieving stated objectives?

- What additional benefits might arise in terms of new direction and opportunity?

- Where would it sit in the present structure in terms of relationships with other activities and areas of responsibility?

- What changes might be necessary in terms of structure and the corporate culture, especially management style?

If answers to this questioning suggest a positive way forward, they can form the basis for a proposed strategy to be put to the organisation at large.

It will be seen from the discussion which follows in Chapter 3 that the amount and complexity of preparation required to pursue knowledge management could seem daunting. In a recent survey, Chase (1997), barriers to the successful creation of knowledge-based organisations were seen as being the organisational culture (80% of respondents), lack of time (60%) and lack of ownership of the problem (64%). It may be that attempting to address all the above issues using existing internal human resources is unrealistic; additional advice may be required. On the other hand, as already indicated, the case for considerable staff involvement is a strong one.

Having made the decision to go ahead, based on wide consultation, it could be useful to call on the services of management consultants to be involved in all or part of the initial preparation and setting up. For example, they could advise on processes and procedures, or recommend software which has been tried and tested for the purpose. They could prepare a manual of procedures (electronic or paper-based) - essential for consistency of approach, especially given the number of people and processes likely to be involved. You may wish the consultants to run a series of seminars as part of the staff consultation and communication process or to assess the skills requirement and design, organise or suggest relevant training and development activities. Whether by your own management or outside consultants, these tasks and others will need to be carried out now and in tandem. They are all interlinked and need to be considered as part of a strategic whole. On this point Chase (1998) says "It is clear from the responses [to questions in his survey] that most of the organisations participating...are approaching Knowledge Management as a series of separate, often unconnected initiatives, rather than from the approach of a holistic business strategy." He also notes the similarity of approach to that seen in the mid-1980s when "companies attempted to introduce aspects of Total Quality Management without addressing the key issue of developing an integrated strategic view of TQM."

There seem to be strong links with a number of other management developments, especially Total Quality Management (TQM) and Business Process Re-engineering (BPR); both aimed at achieving continuous improvement in terms of ensuring efficiency and quality of processes and outputs. They are also dependent on information and on wide-ranging communication and understanding across traditional functional boundaries. The other strong affinity between these and Knowledge Management is the need for ongoing commitment from top management to ensure success. All may be regarded as linchpins of the management of change.

3. GETTING STARTED: INITIAL TASKS

As already indicated, early communication with, and involvement of all those within the organisation is essential. Employees will have concerns about any change, and fears can be allayed by providing enough information about what is proposed and the way it might work, but the final decision-makers should take note not only of concerns, but also of the range of suggestions which may result from the initial consultation process. These may well provide answers to some of the more specific questions that any board, partnership or other form of governing body will also have to address as part of the planning process. Examples of some of these which could well be common to a number of organisations are suggested below, but each organisation is likely to have a variety of other questions to add, relating to their particular responsibilities and objectives, and taking into account any legal or regulatory considerations specific to their sector or industry. It will also be necessary to be aware of the legal implications of knowledge management itself, for example, copyright and licensing. Goodger (1998) provides a useful sumary of these.

Shaping the policy

In addition to the fundamental questions already asked in the previous chapter, there will be others which are concerned with overall policy and structure. For example:

- Who will have overall responsibility for decision-making concerning the future direction of knowledge management?

- Should it be developed on an organisation-wide or a departmental basis?

- If the organisation is international what will the policy be towards providing access to offices worldwide?

- What are the implications for intellectual property rights i.e. who would have ownership of the knowledge once taken into the corporate knowledge base?

- What changes might there need to be regarding the choice and compatibility of technology, both hardware and software?

- Is there a need for a separate knowledge/information policy, that is one which focusses on the content and potential use rather than on the technology?

Decisions regarding the last point will suggest where overall responsibility for knowledge management should rest.

Then there would be some specific questions relating more to operational issues:

- How will the selection, analysis and organisation of the knowledge content be determined?

- How will decisions be made on matters of access and control, and by what means can we ensure appropriate levels of confidentiality and security?

- What about responsibility for the day-to-day operation and maintenance and related decision-making?

- Would additional and focussed IT support be required?

- How appropriate would existing systems applications be, for example, the organisation's intranet?

- Are there other systems and software more suitable for knowledge management which should be considered?

Detailed discussion will be needed as to specific requirements concerning the number of staff and related skills required to support the knowledge management function, the estimated amount of equipment and supporting information sources and services, location, space, and maintenance. As with any other project, initial and ongoing costs will have to be calculated. Procedures will need to be put in place to ensure the efficient collection and organisation of the knowledge content. In particular continuous wide-ranging two-way communication should take place to ensure that a) maximum benefit from individual input is being achieved by building on existing skills, knowledge and experience, b) that individuals are regularly consulted for their views and responses concerning various aspects of the operation and that c) the positive benefits of introducing knowledge management are widely understood and continue to receive support. This process of continuous consultation and feedback should certainly help in achieving the degree of motivation and commitment needed to take the project forward smoothly.

Consultation mechanisms

What mechanisms might be appropriate for the various types and stages of consultation and communication that will need to take place? There are a number of tried and tested methods from which to choose. These are likely to take place via a mixture of face-to-face, paper-based and electronic means and involve a range of different activities. For example, the process may well start with a series of meetings and briefings giving people the opportunity to raise concerns and hopefully have these quickly alleviated, and to seek clarification on points which might have given rise to misunderstanding. It is best to clear away any uncertainties of this kind right at the beginning, providing the climate for a higher degree of early commitment and motivation among the widest possible number of employees. It can help if these meetings contain a mixture of staff of all levels and representing various functions and departments. This can lead to greater understanding as the project progresses, because during the process of questions being raised, individuals will realise that they are not alone in their concerns; others share them. They will learn from each other's questions and increase their understanding not only of the proposed knowledge management function, but also of their colleagues: it could be seen as one of the first steps in bringing about a knowledge-sharing culture.

In addition to these initial exploratory briefings there will be a need for various other types of meetings, some with a particular focus, such as task forces or working parties concerned with specific aspects of development and implementation. The task forces will need to work to an agreed overall schedule, so that progress can be coordinated at each stage of the project. Each participant in these groups could take on responsibility for pursuing a particular element of whatever part of the process is under consideration. Some of the participants will have been selected on account of their known areas of specific activity or knowledge, some for their interpersonal skills, and others for their longstanding knowledge and understanding of the organisation itself. The main aim is to achieve the widest possible range of input. It could well be appropriate in certain areas to make use of some of the existing networks and work teams such as practice groups or project teams. This has the advantage of not requiring new working relationships to be established, although that could have its own downside as people who work together regularly may not necessarily work together well. In other cases it may be preferable to bring together people from different departments and with different areas of expertise. Whatever the final makeup of the group, its members will need to be in regular communication to ensure that any problems are quickly resolved and issues clarified, so that the overall project deadlines are met and the desired outputs for each stage achieved.

Discussion groups of various kinds can be used, including focus groups. The latter are commonly used in market research to test opinion. However the difference between their use in this way and internal use within an organisation is that in external market research the focus group will usually be made up of individuals who are independent of each other, having no formal collective organisational affiliation; whereas in the organisational setting all will be employees and not independent of the company or necessarily of each other. This could influence the responses in terms of the amount of freedom they feel that they have in expressing their opinion, for example in front of their line manager, or the managing director. However that could also apply to other forms of open discussion taking place within the workplace, where these various dependencies exist and where there is not, or has not previously been an open, information-sharing culture.

Another useful consultation mechanism which provides a forum for idea generation, problem-solving and wide-ranging discussion during the early stages of implementation is brainstorming. As its name suggests this operates without a structured agenda but needs be led by an experienced facilitator who is able to encourage creative thinking and draw out new ideas, often on matters which will have a direct effect on the day-to-day operation.

In order to make the most of the outcome of any of these activities, someone needs to record ideas and decisions so that these can be fed into and inform the project as moves forward.

As the project progresses it could be useful to have a series of seminars or presentations by the various working parties or task forces. This would keep people up-to-date with developments and provide further opportunities for clarification and discussion of particular points as they arise. In between these events there could be continuous updating, with information being made available via newsletters or bulletins, both paper-based and electronic, according to the type and purpose of information being provided and response required.

In the case where external consultants or advisors are employed by the organisation, the consultation process may well be carried out by them, but would of course need to involve a number of the organisation's own staff: those who are likely to have key roles in the implementation. Consultants would also be able to advise on the possible alternatives in terms of where the knowledge management operation could best fit into the organisational structure and what structural changes might be required. They would be able to suggest possible options regarding systems and software, taking into consideration the size and business needs of the organisation and the existing systems set-up. They would set out the various processes and procedures necessary for the implementation and the ways in which these would operate. Related to that would be recommendations on the skills which would be needed to support a knowledge management function in its day-to-day operation and maintenance.

At this stage it is likely that the various responsibilities relating to knowledge management will be allocated. This may be as a consequence of advice from any consultants employed, or could be based on expressed interest, expertise already demonstrated by individuals, or as the result of discussions which might have taken place both at board level and during the consultation process. It could be that these various responsibilities will be allocated on a fairly short-term basis at this stage, say for one year, until there is evidence of how it is actually working on the ground, and the type of results it is yielding for the business.

The knowledge audit

Early decisions will have to be made about what the knowledge management function will cover and what to include that will make it a valuable central resource, supporting all the departmental functions and individual work roles within the organisation. A suitable starting point would be to conduct a knowledge audit. The term "audit" traditionally refers to the process by which a company's accounts are formally examined and certified as meeting legal requirements. A more general use of the term is as a methodical examination and review of a situation. The objective of knowledge and information audits is to draw up a picture of the knowledge and information and related systems which exist within an organisation, to see how these support the different functions of the organisation in meeting its overall objectives, and to assess how these might be developed as part of longer-term organisational strategy.

Such audits can then be seen as tools to assist in the process of achieving maximum effective use of all the organisation's intellectual assets. A logical first step could therefore be to draw up an organisational profile, noting the organisation's main aims and objectives, followed by key data concerning its size by number of employees; the number of departments or functions; the number and geographical distribution of sites. This would provide an indication of the potential size and distribution of users of, and contributors to the knowledge function. This would need to be followed by a more detailed survey, department by department and representative of all levels of staff, to establish a) the type of knowledge contribution that each might be able to make and b) the type of knowledge and information to which they might need access in order to perform their role effectively.

The above brief outline indicates the possible approach and intention of a knowledge audit. It is not possible within the constraints of this short guide to go into any detailed discussion of the structure, style, and full range of tools and techniques to be used for such an audit. Their design and use are likely to be determined by the size and spread of the organisation, the experience of those carrying out the exercise, and especially the corporate culture in terms of the degree of openness and willingness to participate, and overall commitment to the concept of knowledge management. However the following key points in conjunction with the above outline should provide a useful framework, and options in terms of methods and techniques which could well be applied to knowledge or information audits can be found in the two publications mentioned elsewhere, Nicholas (1996) and Crawford (1996).

Key points regarding the knowledge audit
- The results of any audit cannot be considered in isolation. To make a full contribution the purpose of the audit and its outcomes must be viewed as part of the overall organisational strategy to put in place a central resource, useful to all.

- Face-to-face interviews seem to offer the most successful method of survey. They provide the opportunity to clarify questions and responses, avoiding ambiguity. However they require careful planning, timing and structure. A well-constructed checklist for the interviewer will help in this.

- In the case of a large organisation it may be that a questionnaire-based survey is seen as more feasible. However this can be used in combination with the face-to-face interview by designating one member of a departmental team to meet with colleagues to discuss the questionnnaire and co-ordinate the views expressed, and highlighting any issues or questions raised. These views can then be discussed in a single face-to-face interview with the co-ordinator but will represent the contributions of a far greater number of people than could be individually interviewed.

- Commitment and positive attitudes throughout the organisation are essential. It seems that demonstrated benefits of any new development are not always enough to get it to take off, as demonstrated in a usability audit carried out by Malde (1992).This looked at the use of e-mail as a means of information dissemination and concluded that at that time it was underused largely due to personal and organisational factors rather than for ergonomic or business reasons. Given preconceived ideas about, and attitudes towards knowledge, information and its management, any audit must be handled with sensitivity. An activity of this kind could be seen as threatening or interfering. It is therefore essential that questions are couched in neutral terms and that the exercise is presented in a positive way, as something which will benefit the whole organisation.

- Potential participants need to be told about the audit, its structure and purpose, with a clear indication of the time likely to be required either for the interview or to complete the questionnaire. It is important that following the final analysis, details of the outcome and its perceived use are fed back to participants and discussed with them. This is likely to generate further ideas for future developments.

- All the activities described above will require those carrying them out to have a clear understanding of the different organisational functions and their purpose, and be underpinned by well-honed communication skills.

- The audit is an extremely valuable tool for planning a new process or activity. But it can also be seen as something for longer-term use and not just as part of the initial stage of implementation. It offers a useful way of regularly updating yourself on what is happening throughout the organisation, keeping in touch with colleagues about their activities and needs, and puts in place a means of wider knowledge- and information-sharing across departments and functions, making it possible to maximise the potential of these assets in achieving the organisation's objectives.

4. NEXT STEPS

Having gone through these initial stages of preparation, made decisions, even if some of these are provisional, and put the necessary infrastructure in place, it could be appropriate to carry out some sort of pilot operation. This would be limited in scope at this stage but would have clear objectives and a set time frame. This would serve the purpose of testing the capability and suitability of systems and software, as well as the capacity of IT support, both internal and external, to cope with the changes in operation; of seeking responses to the new operation, both in terms of demands made and results obtained; of determining the most efficient methods of locating and collecting knowledge; of establishing the most appropriate indexing schemes; of identifying ways of communicating with potential contributors to ensure comprehensiveness of coverage; of devising methods of regular updating. In addition it would be necessary to test the various policy elements of the operation such as those of access and control - are they acceptable and do they work? All those activities will require informed and skilled individuals to manage and monitor each aspect of the new operation. Supervision and assessment of all the tasks involved will be required, with regular feedback to the overall project management group. This will provide continuous review and allow adjustments and changes to be made as required, taking advantage of lessons learned on the way.

Policies should also be shaping up regarding the selection, retention and deletion of items for inclusion in the knowledge database. At the start of the process, perhaps for the duration of any pilot operation, it may well be that the database will be limited to simple listings of a) the subject fields in which knowledge/ expertise is present and b) "expert" individuals within the organisation. The knowledge audit will have suggested key areas likely to be suitable both in the initial stages and later. A decision will also be required at this stage regarding the type and amount of detail to be included in each entry and the length of time for which it might be appropriate to retain the various types of record. As this core resource develops, additional areas are likely to be added, for example, project- or client-related details; notes of relevant and appropriate external experts who can be called upon. A fully-developed knowledge management function is likely eventually to cover a range of other types of information, often by linking in to published external information sources and internally-generated material. An example of this is given in Chapter 9 in the case study of PricewaterhouseCoopers, where a number of interlinked knowledge hubs have been established.

The discussion in the previous paragraph indicates that it is also necessary to consider all existing in-house sources of information along with the current methods of information and records management, looking for possible ways of linking in to these, learning from their "best practice" techniques and liaising over any changes that might be required to co-ordinate the handling and use of knowledge and information as a total organisational resource. As noted in the study of legal firms mentioned earlier, Webb (1996), the existence or proposed development of a know-how function has often led to a review of existing information resources and changes in the way that related services have been delivered.

Interestingly the same study also noted that in addition to IT-based knowledge systems, and other information resources, the personal exchange of knowledge was still rated highly, although in a number of firms this had been formalised beyond the occasional conversation in the corridor, taking place through such events as regular group briefings, project meetings, and training sessions. Other organisations support this approach, especially as the events mentioned are increasingly cross-functional, encouraging wider information exchange and knowledge sharing. In a number of the firms surveyed, the skills of professional librarians and information managers were seen as being a key contributor to the potential success of the know-how function, especially in the areas of structuring and indexing the content for ease and speed of retrieval, where their experience of end-user's needs and information-seeking behaviour was extremely useful. It was also seen as advantageous for library and information staff to conduct training for legal staff in the use of related systems.

Evidence of the required mix of knowledge and skills will start to be provided through the pilot operation as it progresses. It will also suggest the amount and level of authority required to make decisions on a day-to-day basis about what to put in and how best to arrange it for effective use. The research just mentioned showed that, in legal firms at least, the allocation of responsibility for the know-how function (effectively the knowledge managment function) varied considerably. In only 10% of firms did the same person have overall responsibility for the following related areas: know-how activities; IT systems and support; library and information services. Surprisingly in each case that was the Finance Director. In only 4 of the firms surveyed was the title KnowHow Partner used, but in none of these was that the partner's only responsibility. It has been relatively rare for top management, that is at board level, to have included among its job titles a purely knowledge- or information-related post, with the exception of Director of IT. Given the importance now being attached to knowledge management one might expect the focus to change, although the jury is still out on this. A quick scan of recent job advertisements reveals a number which include the word knowledge, either in the job description as part of the list of responsibilities, or in the job title itself. I have noted several calls for "Knowledge Specialists", seemingly at middle management level, which seem to cover anything from research and marketing to telecommunications; and "Knowledge Managers", slightly better paid, with backgrounds in a range of disciplines from management consultancy to business intelligence and information management. So what skills are required to direct, manage and support a knowledge management function? There will be those required to develop strategy (possibly assigned to a member of the top management team along with other responsibilities), those needed for the overall management of the function and those essential to its day-to-day operation. These are discussed in the next chapter.

5. DAY-TO-DAY OPERATION: MANAGEMENT AND RELATED SKILLS

Key tasks and responsibility

Given the discussion so far, it will be apparent that to ensure an efficient and effective knowledge management function which is able to meet its objectives, it is essential to establish precisely which activities will be involved in its day-to-day operation. This will mean listing the various tasks to be done, the frequency with which they need to be carried out, the skills required, and the allocation of responsibilities for their execution.

In addition to a schedule of essential daily tasks, there will be a need for a further listing of other additional tasks relating to the continuous maintenance and development of the knowledge database, or databases, which will be at the heart of the function and which will require regular attention.

Key daily tasks will be:

- collection of new material

- selection for inclusion

- inputting

- indexing

- searching and retrieval

- delivery of output to the end-user.

There will be additional tasks, but those above will be central to the daily operation. Each of the tasks listed above will in turn cover a number of activities and the way in which they are carried out will vary from organisation to organisation. For example, the collection or harnessing of knowledge may be the responsibility of knowledge management staff, or of those who are seen as the knowledge-holders. In a number of businesses the latter process is seen as more likely to bring about the participative, knowledge-sharing culture required. Therefore responsibility for inputting would vary accordingly.

Although a number of different people may be making contributions to the knowledge database by personal inputting, someone has to make a decision about the usefulness or appropriateness of the inclusion of every item put forward. In legal firms this has often been someone with a legal training which would enable them to assess the potential of each record to other lawyers, although the format of record creation along with the choice of indexing methods is usually regarded as something best carried out by the library or information professional.

Often the process of organising the database for most effective retrieval by any specialist user group is the result of consultation and collaboration of legal and information practitioners. In the same setting, other tasks regarded as requiring legal expertise include: writing commentary for any know-how bulletins, analysing the content of legal documents; assessing the importance of certain points in a legal case.

In a different setting those with backgrounds in various disciplines may be trained to carry out what might be regarded as similar tasks, but perhaps not involving such specialist subject knowledge. Library and information service (LIS) staff and others involved in research, regularly write abstracts of reports and journal articles, select or reject items for inclusion in databases, produce bulletins, newsletters and other forms of current awareness and monitoring services.

Knowledge of a wide range of both electronic and other sources, their structure, content, coverage, and level, as well as the most effective way to search them, along with an understanding of the relevance of related software, are other valuable skills which LIS staff are able to bring to knowledge management.

The search process might be a matter of merely seeking a specified record or could involve carrying out more detailed research in response to a general request, perhaps vaguely articulated. In addition to knowing the sources, in whatever format, and how to use them effectively, this will require the researcher to make use of their communication skills in conducting a dialogue through which to establish the enquirer's precise requirement.

Whatever the setting, apart from any specialist subject knowledge requirements, what is most important for the successful operation of knowledge management function is for those involved to have a clear understanding of their broader organisational role. They need to demonstrate an interest in and awareness of activities across the whole organisation and the contribution that they can make to these, and to remain alert to external developments which could influence the organisation and assist them in carrying out their own role within it.

Other regular tasks will include:

- data cleaning & deletion of redundant records

- systems security checks

- setting up links with other internal functions

- creating relevant links with external sources

- updating any manual of procedures specific to the operation.

Again, as with the first list, more tasks could be added according to the corporate setting and again some of these will probably be carried most effectively by cross-discipline or cross-functional collaboration. In the case of the first three tasks above, and possibly in part the fourth, this is likely to be through liaison between the LIS or research staff and the IT support team. It may be that these will start out as joint activities, or that after training could become the longer-term responsibility of one or the other function.

There will also be a need to continually monitor the success of the operation in terms of meeting identified needs. This may in part be carried out as a follow-up to an information needs analysis, usually falling within the remit of the LIS manager. There are a number of ways of evaluating the output of an information service which would well be applied to the knowledge management function. The structure of such evaluations and the necessary tools and techniques to be employed are well-covered in two other titles in this series: Crawford (1996) and Nicholas (1996).

Training end-users in the use of any sources, whatever their format, has long been regarded as part of the role of the LIS or research centre. However it is important to note that however comfortable LIS or research staff may be in using databases themselves, some of them may welcome training in training methods, given the variety available and the different ways in which individuals respond to these.

Keeping up to date

As the above section demonstrates, all the activities mentioned will need to be supported, not only by an appropriate knowledge management policy being in place, but also by relevant training and sound IT support. Equally valuable will be constant two-way communication with all levels of management and regular interaction across disciplines. This will lead to a fruitful cross-fertilisation of ideas and allow maximum coordination of skills and knowledge.

Staff involved in the operation and maintenance of the knowledge core will need to keep themselves up-to-date with what is going on both inside and outside the organisation. Questions to be asked include the following: What new projects are coming on stream? Who is involved? Which additional areas of business might the organisation be considering? Are there any activities in which it might cease to be involved? In the wider marketplace, what are its competitors doing? Answers to such questions will determine the content requirement of databases within the knowledge management function.

There will also be a need to keep up-to-date with new ways of organising information in terms of creating records and making the most of indexing tools; learning about new software products and evaluating them for particular tasks. Wherever possible join the user groups which relate to specific products; this will provide you with a network of contacts with whom to raise questions, exchange experiences and discuss areas of common concern. It will also provide a powerful voice with which to lobby the producers of such products if you experience any problems. Read the relevant journals, and follow up leads. From the Website to the newsletter with telephone and face-to-face communication in between, you will be building up an invaluable personal network and support resource, as well as having the means to acquire further knowledge yourself.

Summary of required skills and competencies

The above section will already have indicated the different types of skills that those working in the knowledge management function will need. They are as much about the ability to interact and communicate effectively as about organising and using information of all kinds. As the PricewaterhouseCoopers case study clearly shows in its framework of competencies, business awareness and the ability to work with others are equally as important as research and analysis skills.

Anyone working in the field of knowledge and information management will require a range of skills which could be grouped under two headings. In the two lists which follow, the skills shown under the first heading are concerned with day-to-day work management and although essential to those working in a knowledge-focussed department, would apply to most other disciplines; those under the second are more specific to activities related to knowledge and information management.

General day-to-day operational skills

- **understanding of the organisation's**
  - business & activities
- **computer applications**
  - word processing
  - graphics
  - spreadsheets
  - CD-ROMs
  - online/networks/email
- **interpersonal skills**
- **oral communication**
- **written communication**
  - appropriate style
  - presentation
- **personal work management**
  - use of time
  - assigning priorities
  - recording results
  - meeting deadlines
- **management**
  - planning
  - decision making
  - human resources
  - finance
- **organisational involvement**

Knowledge & information management skills

- **knowledge of sources**
  - print/electronic
  - internal/external
  - who to ask
  - how to look
  - evaluation
- **subject knowledge & understanding**
- **information & records management**
  - indexing methods
  - database development
  - thesaurus construction
  - retrieval/delivery methods
  - electronic storage
  - retention policy
  - structuring records
  - legislation, standards & controls
- **networks (internal/external)**
- **users/patterns of usage**
  - needs analysis
  - satisfaction measures
- **current awareness services**
  - monitoring/updating
  - abstracting
  - news services e.g. via bulletins, Websites
- **user advice & training**
- **contribution to knowledge & information strategy**

Whilst not everyone will be expected to have all these skills in place when taking on a role in knowledge management, the above lists will suggest areas for training and will assist in setting objectives for longer-term personal development. In the UK, recognition of the national importance of developing appropriate underpinning skills to support knowledge management activity has been shown by the Library & Information Commission through its research initiative. This is in the form of an investigation into the LIS training implications of knowledge management. The Commission is a public body whose function is to advise the UK Government on library and information issues.

In the USA the Special Libraries Association has been organising training events and conference sessions as well as publishing regularly articles on the subject in its journal Information Outlook. The Australian Library and Information Association has also demonstrated its active interest in similar ways, especially through the work of its various sections and related groups. Contact details for these organisations are given with others in the Appendix.

6. SYSTEMS AND SOFTWARE

It is not the intention of this guide to recommend particular systems or software packages. Firstly, because new and increasingly sophisticated packages are coming onto the market all the time. What might be recommended today may have been replaced tomorrow - such is the nature of technology and the pace of change. Secondly, because organisations need to take into account their overall IT requirements and coordinate the needs of all functions including those of knowledge management accordingly. Therefore their choice of systems and software must suit their overall strategy.

However, it is worth making the following general comments and mentioning one or two products in use by particular types of organisation or for specific purposes:

- in some organisations the aim has been to try and establish one IT set-up for all internal applications including knowledge management and document management; in others there has been a preference to keep the document management system separate from knowledge management and other internal IT uses, especially with the increase in cross-organisation networking. This rather depends on the type of business in which the organisation is involved and the amount of confidential or sensitive material that is regularly handled as part of this;

- increasing use is being made of intranets for knowledge management, with appropriate security safeguards in terms of access and control. LIS managers to whom I have spoken have indicated that they have moved on from tailormade packages to using the intranet supported by various off-the-shelf software products for knowledge management. As indicated above this has meant in some cases separating it from the organisation's document management system. Some examples of the use of intranets in knowledge management are given in a survey of their use by Basker (1998);

- tried and tested "groupware" products such as Lotus Notes are still widely used, especially in management consulting firms and legal firms of which an example is also given in Basker's survey. Another product which has been in use for some time and is still seen as appropriate for knowledge management use is Idealist, a text database manager which works under Windows, providing a facility to link into word processing applications. For example, one user runs the organisation's list of experts' C.V.s on the back of it, as well other lists and finds that it works well. To quote this same longstanding Idealist user "If you know it, and it works - why change it?" This was one of the products identified in the survey, Webb (1996), as in use by small and medium sized legal firms, not least because in addition to other facilities it provides the means of linking into the databases of Legal Information Resources, which also uses Idealist. There are a number of other products around which could be equally suitable;

- demands made of today's products are for systems that will talk to each other, efficient back-up from producers, facilities which will allow a wide range of applications and the ability to link quickly and easily into both internal and external networks and databases;

- those developing a core of knowledge databases can find it useful to construct a thesaurus of common terms to be used across all the internal databases to ensure consistency of approach and comprehensive retrieval. For those unfamiliar with thesaurus construction or needing to remind themselves of basic principles, the third edition of the standard work by Aitchison, Gilchrist & Bawden (1997) will provide helpful and practical guidance;

- evaluate new products by: talking to personal contacts in other organisations, reading product reviews, going to the numerous exhibitions and conferences and trying out the products on show, or get a demonstration diskette of any product which looks to be a likely candidate for your particular requirements. Above all, discuss your particular needs with the central technical department of your organisation and coordinate planning to ensure compatibility and the availibility of in-house technical support;

- finally, there is a danger that IT will become the driver rather than the tool. Select your systems and software to do the job that needs to be done, in the way that will be most effective for your organisation. Sistla and Todd (1998) utter warnings about doing otherwise, particularly when creating a knowledge-centred resource.

7. MEASURING THE VALUE OF KNOWLEDGE

How do you measure something as seemingly incapable of being measured as knowledge? If knowledge is regarded as being of such value to the success of an organisation, how can that value be expressed in terms of its actual worth? Over the years various techniques have been put forward for measuring the efficiency of information services, such as performance measures, but concrete measures of the actual value of the information provided have not been as readily available. Currently a number of libraries are looking at the use of benchmarking as a means of measuring the effectiveness of services and developing 'best practice' benchmarks. Problems in assessing value have been experienced in the setting-up of fee-based information services when making pricing decisions. Badenoch *et al.* (1994) offer a useful discussion of the various models which have been used in the LIS field, noting particularly the difficulties in applying techniques such as cost-benefit analysis to information. If that has been the case, at least until recently, of attempting to assign value to information, can the situation be any different in the case of knowledge?

Things have moved on. Knowledge and information are certainly intangibles, but there are ways of assessing their value. To take a simple example: in the corporate LIS setting, it has been a useful practice to seek regular structured feedback in terms of the satisfaction levels of users. This may relate to the relevance and completeness of material provided (quality); to the way it was presented and delivered (helpfulness); and to the speed and appropriateness of the method of delivery (timeliness). These are often placed on a satisfaction index based on a ranking of, say, 1-5. Whilst these may still be seen as being difficult to measure in traditional terms, factors such as the time saved on the part of the end-user and the actual contribution to overall organisational activity might be seen as lending themselves more to measurement.

These are examples of simple indicators with which a number of LIS practitioners will already be familiar, through having conducted user satisfaction surveys, perhaps as follow-ups to information audits and needs analyses, as discussed elsewhere. Urquhart & Hepworth (1995) have drawn up a toolkit of guidelines and methods which can be used not only to assess information needs, but also to help assess the value of the outcomes to the ultimate use of information provided.

Although these were drawn up with health libraries in mind, this would seem to be a useful tool on which to build, especially where the LIS has a role in both information and knowledge management; in fact the authors recommend that the toolkit be revised and adapted to local need.

The use of non-financial measures

To return to the broader subject of measuring the value of the total corporate knowledge resource as an asset. There are of course accounting standards which relate to the treatment of intangible assets such as goodwill, but as Sveiby (1997) suggests, conventional accounting based on the use of financial indicators to assess a company's value and indicate its future worth, is probably not as appropriate in terms of measuring the state of a company whose main assets are its people. This view is supported by Hope & Hope (1997) who contend that "in many organisations the strategic direction and the budgeting system are contradictory" and that "managers are measured on their own piece of the hierarchy rather than on their contribution to strategic objectives".

Hamel (1995) noted that in a world where knowledge is central, a company's value in terms of its intellectual assets, is not shown on the balance sheet. As he says "there is no funds flow statement for knowledge." However Robinson & Kleiner (1996) writing only a year later were discussing measurement and valuation techniques to be applied to intellectual capital, which they saw as not only relating to intellectual property concepts such as patents and licences, but also to less tangible assets like know-how, skills and information systems. At the same Lester (1996) was describing the move by the Swedish financial services group, Skandia, which was already publishing an "intellectual capital report" as a supplement to its annual report. This company has since become widely known for its lead in that direction and has moved on to develop, with Leif Edvinsson, a formal measurement system for the purpose: the Skandia Navigator.

Sveiby devotes three chapters of his book to discussing the reasons for moving away from financial indicators, outlining a series of specific measures which can be used and describing the ways in which these have been tested in several different companies and different sectors. He has developed a series of indicators by which to consider corporate effectiveness in terms of competence, internal structure and external structure, and offers several possible indicators for each. These are described with examples in chapters 12 and 13 of his book.

Sveiby has developed his Intangible Assets Monitor, based on the chapters in his book mentioned above. He has also developed a business simulation to be run as a two-day workshop to assist participants in learning to apply a knowledge-focussed strategy to manage and measure knowledge-based assets. Incidentally in this same book Sveiby invites those interested in continuing the dialogue on knowledge management generally to visit his Web site (contact details in the Appendix).

The IMPACT Programme, whose Board Agenda questions are listed in Chapter 2, has now also developed a diagnostic tool, the Health Information Index, which can be used to objectively assess an organisation's performance with respect to those ten questions. Recognising the importance of creating value, IMPACT's latest work is focussed on creating a set of similar questions and a diagnostic tool with which to assess an organisation's capability to exploit information and knowledge assets.

Intellectual capital management and the ways in which it has been put into practice in a number of companies is discussed by Sullivan (1998). Elsewhere, other measures have been also been tested and a variety of new measurement methods have emerged. These, with examples of their use, are described and evaluated in a comprehensive research report on measuring the value of knowledge, Skyrme (1998).

All those measures mentioned above are well worth exploring in more detail, as it seems that the non-financial indicator will certainly be the one most widely used in assessing the value of knowledge as an organisational asset.

8. CONCLUSIONS

As has been indicated the ways of managing knowledge are still being explored and tested. There is still more to learn. However the key components of a possible strategy are likely to stand for some time. These are as follows:

- The corporate culture will be the key contributor to success in implementing a knowledge management policy. It needs to be open and participative taking account of knowledge, skills and ideas which exist throughout the organisation. This will be based on continuous consultation and feedback at all levels. *Involve, not impose*, must be the watchword.

- Organisations of today and of the future are only likely to reap the full benefits from their investment in resources if they build knowledge management into their strategic planning. As with any other development which aims to improve overall organisational performance, it should not be undertaken in a piecemeal fashion, but as part of a coordinated policy.

- Knowledge management is part of the management of change. As well as changing the corporate culture, related changes, for example, in working practices, as well as in IT, need to be taken into account in developing the knowledge management function. Change should be presented as opportunity rather than threat and managed accordingly.

- Not all things will have to change completely; it is useful to build on existing strengths. Make the most of procedures and processes that work and could form a valuable basis for the new development; identify and make full use of existing skills.

- Knowledge management needs to be supported by appropriate systems and procedures, along with relevant skills, training and development programmes and continuous monitoring.

- Learning from the experience of others, such as that described in the case studies which follow in the next chapter, can be invaluable. Bringing in outside assistance and advice where necessary, for example, from consultants who specialise in this area, can also save a lot of time and help avoid what could be seen as "re-inventing the wheel" activity.

- Financial indicators are no longer considered to be the only way of measuring an organisation's worth. Consider new ways of measuring the value of intellectual assets. In terms of cost versus value, the question is not, do you need knowledge management, but rather, can you do without it?

- Ketelhohn (1996) suggests that the key to successful management lies in thinking, but notes that creating what he describes as management toolboxes has often been seen as a way to solve management problems, avoiding the need to think them through. He says that "The assumption behind this is that it would allow managers to produce instant solutions to complex problems". He argues that understanding does not come from using tools, it comes from education, thereby underlining the importance of recognising the role of knowledge in an organisation. As he so aptly puts it "Toolboxes are out, thinking is in".

The above summary of key points seeks to underline the importance of developing a knowledge management culture in which organisations can fully realisse their intellectual assets. Practical examples of the ways in which organisations can fully realise their intellectual assets. Practical examples of the ways in which three large organisations have set about this are described in the chapter which follows. I am grateful to those organisations for their willingness to share their experiences, and in doing so demonstrate the possible benefits of becoming a knowledge-centred organisation.

9. CASE STUDIES

1 - The PricewaterhouseCoopers Information and Knowledge Exchange (IKE)

Chris Cooper, Knowledge Centre Manager

Introduction

Management Consultancy is one of the best examples of a knowledge-based business. The knowledge and skills of our consultants are our only enduring asset. As a knowledge based business, an effective knowledge management programme is of critical importance to us. In order to be effective as a major consultancy, knowledge management must help us address a number of key business challenges:

- When advising clients our consultants must be able to draw not just on their own knowledge, but that of our entire business.

- Our clients are leading global businesses. They expect from us a consistent approach wherever in the world we work with them.

- Staff turnover is typically 15% or more per year. Our new joiners must be fully effective from day one.

- We want our best people to progress through our organisation as quickly as possible. Constant access to our corporate knowledge base helps them to develop their skills rapidly.

- Constantly changing markets necessitate continuous updating of the servicelines we sell and the dissemination of new developments to all our staff.

- We are an organisation which has recently embraced merger. The knowledge management systems of our two predecessor organisations are enabling us to develop a new corporate knowledge base with maximum effect.

The Information and Knowledge Exchange (IKE) was developed to address these challenges by making knowledge of our servicelines, our clients, the industry sectors we work in, our past proposals and past client assignments available to all our employees. It is an essential tool for all our people. Development and launch of IKE took place within the UK firm of Coopers & Lybrand prior to the recent merger with Price Waterhouse, a user population of some 1600 people.

The title of IKE was deliberately chosen to include both the terms 'information' and 'knowledge'. In common with many other knowledge management systems, IKE supports the sharing of a great deal of information and some knowledge.

The Information and Knowledge Exchange (IKE)

The Information and Knowledge Exchange consists of both dedicated human resources and a Lotus Notes based knowledge management system. The main focus of this case study is on the human resources and the skills that they require. However, in order to create a context for these skills it is first necessary to outline the scope of IKE.

IKE is designed to support the key business processes of PricewaterhouseCoopers Management Consultancy Services (MCS). These processes are listed in Table 1.

Business Profile	Supporting IKE Applications
Develop Servicelines	Serviceline Development
Manage Key Client Ccounts	Account Management
Win Business	Sales and Leads Tracking Proposal Support
Deliver Assignments	Assignment Support
Manage People	CVs and Skills Library Personnel List Courses and Bookings

Table 1: Key business processes and corresponding IKE process support applications

The first main element of IKE is a set of groupware tools which support consultants in carrying out these processes. These are listed in the right hand column of Table 1.

Typically the consultants engaged in the key processes of Figure 1 require access to existing sources of information and are in turn generating new information. For example, a team putting together a proposal will require access to past proposals, similar assignments, marketing material for the relevant serviceline, information about the client and CV's etc. The team produce a new client proposal which may be of use to others bidding for similar pieces of work in the future. This information which is used in a business process, or produced by a business process, is stored in a comprehensive suite of knowledge libraries which make up the second key component of IKE. These support all servicelines and market sectors and also include libraries of past proposals, assignment experience statements and materials specific to key client accounts.

The third and arguably most critical element of IKE is the knowledge hub network. A knowledge hub has responsibility for the sharing of a key area of knowledge. It will have one or more full-time dedicated staff working within it who are responsible for supporting IKE knowledge sharing applications.

The knowledge hubs

Our knowledge hubs fall into three types:

- Serviceline hubs – supporting one or more of our servicelines (examples of our servicelines would be change management, corporate strategy development, financial systems implementation etc).

- Sector hubs – supporting a key sector (examples would be financial services, health, pharmaceuticals and chemicals etc).

- Client account hubs – supporting a major client account team.

Establishing a successful knowledge management system such as IKE requires major change in the business operation. The activities involved include the following:

- Gaining and maintaining sponsorship from senior management.

- Communicating the requirements and benefits of knowledge management at all levels in the organisation.

- Development and implementation of network based knowledge sharing applications.

- Training and support of users in how and when to access the system to locate information.

- Training and support of users in how and when to contribute knowledge to applications.

- Managing the organisation and quality of content.

- Research to supplement content and to support user needs.

- The knowledge hubs have a vital role to play in all of these activities.

Organisation of the knowledge hubs

The knowledge hubs are essential to the success of our knowledge management programme. Given the breadth of their role it is essential that any individual working in the hub is assigned to the role full-time – this is not a role that can be undertaken by a consultant in between client assignments, or by a secretary as a spare time activity. The resources allocated to hubs are designated 'knowledge hub managers' and 'knowledge hub assistants' and are all full-time.

In order to support our user population of 1600 we have six hubs covering the range of industry sectors we work in, eight supporting the sevicelines we sell to clients and a generic hub for general MCS news and information. In addition to these, we have a number of full-time hub managers supporting major client account teams. Some hubs consist of a single full-time person. The largest hubs contain a hub manager and up to three assistants.

The knowledge hubs provide an essential service to the business, and in order to maximise business contact and accountability the staff in any hub are 'owned' and managed by the most appropriate sector or serviceline business group.

In addition to the knowledge hubs, we maintain a knowledge centre which is a corporate group. The role of the knowledge centre is to co-ordinate the knowledge management programme, including the development of tools, methods of working, policies etc and to develop the knowledge hub network. These roles are summarised in Table 2.

Organisational Unit	Role	Resources
Knowledge Centre	Deliver tools, techniques, policies, working methods and training. Monitor success of programme	Chief Knowledge Officer Knowledge Centre Assistant Manager Trainer Administrator
1 Generic Knowledge Hub 6 Sector Hubs 8 Serviceline Hubs 4 Account Hubs	User support Implement Knowledge Centre policies Feed back to Knowledge Centre on issues, problems, requirements	19 Hub Managers 15 Hub Assistants

Table 2: Roles in the knowledge management organisation

Key requirements of the knowledge hub role

Overall the knowledge hub role consists of the following five key elements:

- Maintaining the content of IKE libraries.
- Maintaining libraries of hard copy materials.
- Supporting users of IKE.
- Undertaking research.
- Knowledge sharing evangelism.

(i) Maintaining the content of IKE libraries

The hub team is required to locate relevant materials which they either add to the library or encourage a consultant to add directly. Our aim is to have users adding documents wherever possible. New additions are monitored and checked for content, relevance etc. A categorisation scheme must be established and periodically reviewed. Good abstracts are required, both to save user time when assessing the relevance of documents, and also to enable the search function to locate relevant documents which are held as attached word processor, presentation or spreadsheet files.

The needs of users who have very little time must be paramount, and our objective is that they should be able to locate relevant materials in the electronic libraries with minimum effort. The hub manager must make every effort to guide users to the most relevant material by creating categorisation schemes which are easy to understand, by building 'guided tour' overview documents and by removing material which is out of date or causes unnecessary duplication.

Design and maintenance of a virtual library requires specific disciplines including arrangement of documents so that they can be understood when viewed within the confines of a PC screen, minimising the amount of user 'drill down' and scrolling, and providing clear information about the size and content of attached documents.

(ii) Maintaining libraries of hard copy materials

Our objective is to provide virtual libraries wherever possible. However our knowledge hubs still have to manage hard copy materials for a number of reasons:

- Copyright law prevents the electronic distribution of most external materials such as books, journal articles, conference proceedings etc.

- Marketing brochures and publications must be held as hard copy.

- Some of our legacy material is only available as hard copy. Scanning may be too time-consuming or in some cases would result in excessively large bitmaps files that would greatly increase the size of our virtual libraries.

- Increasingly the hubs need to handle other formats such as videos, equipment for business games and facilitated exercises.

These items are indexed in the virtual library with a button provided which enables a user to email the hub manager and request the loan of the relevant item. The library records the loan and the subsequent return. Provision of this service necessitates a reference system so that hard copy materials can be located quickly.

It is especially important that a good abstract is created in the virtual library for each hard copy document so that these can be located by the search function and also so that users can assess whether the material is relevant to them.

(iii) Supporting users of IKE

User training in the use of any computer application is of key importance. Lotus Notes is our preferred tool for knowledge sharing and no user is allowed a Notes ID until s/he has undergone a one day training course. Our 'IS (Information Systems) Right Skills' training programme has been used to benchmark the IT skills of all our employees in the use of our standard office suite (word processor, presentation package, spreadsheet etc) and training is supplied to enable everyone to attain the target skill level.

Training in the use of the IKE applications has been given to every new member of staff who has joined the firm in the past three years. This includes an overview of the components of IKE, how to locate information, how to contribute information and how to get help from the hub manager network and the knowledge centre. Even though a well structured training programme is provided we still find that there is a surprisingly wide variation in levels of IT literacy. Some of the difficulties users face include problems in remembering all the information that is presented during training courses, forgetting how to carry out simple tasks due to infrequent use and lack of confidence with unfamiliar technology.

Hub managers regularly provide supplementary training to their users in the use of IKE and are required to assist users in understanding the basic functionality of any IKE application.

(iv) Undertaking research

Research covers a wide range of requirements. Requests may be as diverse as the following:

- How many languages are spoken in Europe and the Middle East?

- Summarise our previous world-wide experience of finance function outsourcing assignments.

- What predictions are being made for growth of the European digital video disc market?

A basic enquiry might be resolved immediately and an answer provided over the telephone. At the other end of the scale a major research assignment could take several days or weeks of work to complete and culminate in the presentation of results to an external client of the firm by the researcher. Our hub managers who do not have an information science background are not expected to undertake major pieces of research, and certainly not without substantial training and career development. Even the handling of quite straight-forward requests requires the development of new skills.

The first new skill is that of taking time to question the customer and ensure that the requirement has been correctly understood. Quite often the real need may be somewhat different from what is initially asked for. Secondly, it is important to understand that the customer requires quality of information rather than quantity. For example, a request for information about activity based costing almost certainly should be met with the definitive overview document, and not with a list of 30 assorted documents in the general subject area.

An understanding of available sources, both internal and external, is essential, as is familiarity with the terminology and concepts of the subject area. Effective handling of large numbers of requests requires skills in time management, prioritisation and the self confidence to explain to the customer what can and cannot be realistically achieved in the time available. Written reports require skills in writing clearly and concisely.

Hub personnel should constantly seek to add business value in the services they provide. Examples include providing summaries and interpretation of content in order to save customer time, directing the customer to information other than that which is directly requested but which could be very relevant to the customer need and providing targeted alerting services.

(v) Knowledge sharing evangelism

Achieving success in a knowledge management initiative is above all about culture change. It is about persuading individuals of the benefits to be gained from sharing their personal knowledge (including that held in heads, in filing cabinets and on computer disks) with their colleagues openly and willingly. Winning the argument that knowledge sharing is a 'good thing' is only half the battle. Busy people must be convinced that knowledge sharing is equally as important as client work and they must be given a clear understanding of what is expected and the milestones in their project where knowledge should be shared.

Knowledge hub managers are essential agents in the change programme and must be prepared to actively promote the message of knowledge sharing within their user groups. They cannot be expected to achieve change on their own, and must be backed by strong sponsorship and by organisation-wide initiatives including incorporation of knowledge sharing activity into the appraisal and promotion criteria of consultants. The knowledge hub manager will often need to convince business leaders in his or her part of the organisation of the importance of knowledge sharing as a first step to gain local sponsorship before attempting to influence the behaviour of the consultants. The hub team must develop a programme for building a knowledge sharing culture which is tailored to the needs of their business group.

Previous careers of knowledge hub specialists

In general PwC knowledge hub staff come from one of two backgrounds:

Qualified information scientists who were previously designated 'researchers' by the business. Prior to the development of IKE, researchers worked primarily with external information resources, and carried out research to support proposal preparation and client assignment teams.

Senior secretarial staff who have extensive knowledge of the business and are looking for a new career direction.

Adopting the knowledge hub role

All those accepting a knowledge hub role faced some degree of challenge in adapting to the new role. In order to be successful it was necessary for them to develop new skills and to broaden their knowledge of the business. As a first step all of them needed to develop an understanding of knowledge management.

Researchers were in some cases reluctant to become involved in the management of internal information because their training and previous careers had been focused predominantly on the use of external sources of information. Some had a concern that involvement in the management of internal information was of little value to their career development.

In practice, researchers had to raise their profile within the business and become much more proactive than before. They were required to actively promote the use of IKE, to evaluate the training needs of their user communities and to find ways of encouraging consultants to contribute assignment learning and key documents to the knowledge sharing libraries. The increased visibility in the business has aided their career development.

For secretarial staff the initial challenge was that of moving to a role where they had to decide how to allocate their time. Work no longer piled up in the in-tray continuously. Instead they had to manage their time so that they both met immediate user requests and developed the content of the virtual libraries, maintained their own current awareness and understanding and provided the necessary training and support to enable consultants to use and contribute to the applications. Secretarial staff have been required to learn basic research and analysis skills in which they had no previous training.

Overall we have found that the most important differentiator between success and failure of an individual as a hub manager has been that of personality with the ability to act on personal initiative an essential attribute. Strong outgoing personalities, whether from an information science or secretarial background, have been the most successful. Quieter personalities have more difficulty in maintaining credibility with consultants, in promoting the message of knowledge sharing and in the persistence and follow-through which is necessary to obtain the learning summaries, reports and presentations required to keep the knowledge sharing applications up to date.

The hub manager competency framework

Competency frameworks are used widely in our business as a means for individuals and line managers to assess current skills and identify areas for further development. We have designed a Knowledge and Information Management (KIM) Competency Framework for our hub managers and assistants for this purpose. At the present time the emphasis is on self-assessment and personal development. A more formal assessment process based on the existing framework but using 360° feedback may be implemented at a future date.

The idea of a competency framework is to set out the behaviours and activities required in order to fulfil a role. The emphasis is on observable behaviour so that 'has attended a training course on abstracting' is not a competency but 'writes concise informative abstracts' is.

Within our framework the following seven competencies are defined:

- **Working with Others:** working with others internal and external to PwC, both in a supervisory and non-supervisory role. Possession of strong interpersonal skills. Ability to understand feelings, motivations and behaviours of others. Communicates through listening, orally and in writing.

- **IT Skills:** the use of software products and electronic media to enhance work processes and ensure the efficient transfer of information.

- **Planning & Organisation:** the ability to effectively prioritise activities and approach tasks in a structured and organised manner.

- **Business Awareness:** understands the nature of the consulting practice including its organisational structure, key processes, servicelines, markets and business strategy.

- **Providing the Service/User Focus:** uses a knowledge of user needs together with a comprehensive understanding of information and technical resources to deliver a high quality, flexible and responsive service. Contributes to the development and roll-out of the Serviceline/Sector/Account offering.

- **Research & Analysis Skills:** uses a knowledge of resources and analytical skills to deliver timely, high quality, focused results to both the consulting community and clients.

- **Promoting Knowledge Management:** acts as knowledge sharing 'evangelist' promoting the positive aspects of the knowledge sharing culture at all levels.

For each of the seven competencies a table is constructed which lists relevant behaviours at four levels of competence. The levels of competence are:

- **Level 1 (Awareness):** applies the competency in routine situations.

- **Level 2 (Practitioner):** applies the competency in demanding situations.

- **Level 3 (Expert):** applies the competency in challenging, unusual or highly sensitive situations.

- **Level 4 (Guru):** acts as a point of reference within the firm, people go out of their way to seek their advice.

Research & Analysis Skills	Level of Competence			
Definition	1 (Awareness)	2 (Practitioner)	3 (Expert)	4 (Guru)
Uses a knowledge of resources and analytical skills to deliver timely, high quality, focused results to both the consulting community and clients	Uses IKE to assist client proposal/assignment support or refers user to appropriate Knowledge Hub or Account Hub	Retrieves accurate material from across MCS to support client proposal/assignment unaided	Evaluates and selects relevant material from across PwC to support client proposal/assignment. Uses PwC IT systems and staff contacts nationally	Develops client proposal, evaluates and selects material for client proposal/assignment
	Retrieves relevant raw material according to detailed brief.	Retrieves relevant raw material according to an outline brief.	Develops PwC personal contacts internationally	Writes client proposal/report in part/whole
	Drafts reports as directed	Delivers complete, relevant reports, translating jargon, where appropriate, into layman's terms	Assists user to develop brief and retrieves relevant material. Tailors raw data (textual or numerical) to meet request	Develops brief and identifies additional relevant material
	Presents data in a clear, logically structured and organised manner	Reviews media/locates items relevant to assignments or general interest with some guidance	Reviews media and locates relevant items unaided. Provides regular current awareness service	Interprets and draws conclusions from raw data applying statistical analysis where appropriate
	Retrieves requested items from specified media	Retrieves external business information from external sources with some assistance	Develops knowledge of external information sources using various formats & personal knowledge contacts	Evaluates new external sources of information. Assesses value, including cost benefit analysis. Provides business case for new information sources
	Uses PwC libraries for external business information	Evaluates and summarises large quantities of data and identifies key issues in line with user/client needs	Evaluates & selects best source of external information dependent on time/cost/format	Monitors sector/industry developments and assesses impact on PwC and identifies potential selling opportunities
			Evaluates & selects relevant material for specialised external information collection	Applies extensive knowledge of sector/industry specific external information sources
				Evaluates new external sources of information and promotes usage

Table 3: Behaviours for the Research & Analysis Skills Competency

Table 3 shows the behaviours for the 'Research & Analysis Skills' competency. The other six competencies which go to make up the full framework for knowledge hub managers and assistants are similar in format.

Hub manager training

In order to be effective as a means of personal development a competency framework must provide details of learning routes for the behaviours defined. Learning can take several forms including in-house and off-site training courses, learning on the job, training videos and computer-based training. Each competency table, such as that shown in table 3, is supported by a table of learning routes.

Given that many of the hub managers do not have an information science background, the training provision for the Research & Analysis Skills competency has been of particular importance. Guided by this framework a training scheme has been developed in conjunction with external trainers to underpin the core skills of this competency. This has provided a basic grounding in the following areas:

- Overview of knowledge management.
- The role of the information unit.
- Organising information.
- Offering a current awareness service.
- Using IT.
- External information sources.
- Desk research.
- Writing concisely and abstracting.
- Handling enquiries.

Further organised training is planned to underpin this and other competencies, but individuals have a responsibility to manage their own training programmes guided by the competency framework.

Conclusions

A number of lessons can be drawn from the experience of developing and implementing IKE:

- A knowledge management programme is a wide-ranging initiative requiring the enactment of substantial business change.

- Full-time dedicated resource is required to assist in the implementation of this change and to ensure that the knowledge sharing programme is sustained. The major part of this resource takes the form of hub managers and hub assistants who manage the capture and organisation of information, train and support users and above all communicate and encourage the need to openly share information.

- IKE has drawn on a mixed community from both information scientists and senior secretarial roles to acts as agents of this change.

- These 'hub managers' and 'hub assistants' have been well received by the business and are making a major contribution to the success of the IKE initiative.

- All hub managers, irrespective of career background, have needed to learn new skills in order to be successful in the role.

- The competency framework and associated training courses and learning aids have supported the development of the necessary skills.

- Although most individuals have required development in some areas, the over-riding ingredient for success has been in the area of interpersonal skills where a strong pro-active and outgoing personality is very important irrespective of qualifications and previous experience.

- A knowledge sharing programme such as IKE requires strong support from senior management.

- If success is to be achieved then all employees must understand the benefits of knowledge management to the organisation and must make a contribution to knowledge sharing.

2 - Valuing ICL knowledge

Valuing ICL Knowledge: A case study

Elizabeth Lank, Programme Director, Mobilising Knowledge, ICL

Background
ICL is an international company of 19,000 people, focused on helping its customers seize the opportunities of the Information Age. ICL was established in 1968 as a computer designer and manufacturer. Over the last ten years the company has been transforming itself into a service-led organisation whose knowledge **about** technology is its real asset. This transformation has made it a strategic imperative for ICL to excel at leveraging its intellectual capital across the world. This case study shares the approach taken and some of the lessons so far, with a particular emphasis on some of the new roles that we believe knowledge-based businesses will need to establish.

Building the business case

In 1994 ICL was already well along the path to becoming a service-led organisation. There was a growing awareness that this intangible thing called knowledge was a vital asset that was not being leveraged as effectively as it might. What were some of the symptoms of this?

• Duplication of effort in developing new services and methodologies.

• Several ICL businesses unknowingly bidding for the same customer projects.

• Difficulty in quickly identifying company experts to support projects.

An informal group of interested ICL people met in late 1994, calling itself the Knowledge Management Network. We very soon realised that a great deal of knowledge management happened already within the organisation - for example, we identified 23 different internal information services for employees. However, because these were entirely uncoordinated, there was much duplication of effort even within these services. Also, many activities were being undertaken by well-meaning individuals who were doing it to be helpful, without enough time, budget or management support to really make a significant difference to the business. As it met throughout 1995, the group became increasingly convinced of the importance of the issue. In Keith Todd's first week as Chief Executive of ICL in January 1996, the business case was put to him to appoint a full-time programme director for a cross-company initiative in this area. He accepted the business case and Project VIK (Valuing ICL Knowledge) was born.

Deciding where to start

The intellectual capital of an organisation is an invisible yet crucial asset. As Thomas Stewart has put it, "Trying to identify and manage knowledge assets is like trying to fish barehanded. It can be done... but the object of the effort is damnably elusive." In the early weeks of Project VIK, it became clear that there were three significant areas that would need to be influenced in order to make an impact. These were

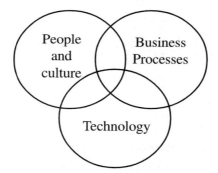

Fig. 1

We felt that a clear understanding was needed of these different areas and that the best way to achieve this was to form a small catalyst team with a mix of cross-functional skills. The advertisement of these Project VIK opportunities on ICL's global e mail system generated 120 responses from 14 different countries. The interest and challenge of the project had clearly struck a chord. By mid 1996 the small Project VIK catalyst team (five people in total) was formed with a breadth of experience represented within it.

We quickly appreciated the opportunity that new technologies (e.g. intranet and groupware) brought to make information and knowledge visible to a global community. We decided that creating a global information service for employees on ICL's intranet could be an early win. Such a service could make a quick impact on productivity by reducing the time people waste trying to find company information. Named Café VIK, with 'Café' chosen to reinforce the idea of connecting people, this service was selected as the first major deliverable of Project VIK.

Developing Café VIK

In a world where information overload is becoming a serious issue, it might seem counter-productive to focus on providing even more information. Yet effective services that bring the right information to people on a just-in-time basis can actually give people back a precious commodity - time. Our client managers estimated that they spent up to one day in five seeking information and expertise. If we could cut that searching time down by even 50%, it would be a significant productivity enhancement, freeing up their time to add greater value to their clients.

With this goal of freeing up unproductive time in mind, we ran a number of focus groups for front-line employees - consultants, project managers, salespeople who dealt directly with our customers. The question we asked them was simple: what information do you need to do your job effectively? Although they represented a broad range of ICL business units, some clear direction came through from them. They made it clear that they needed:

- information about ICL itself so that they could be effective ambassadors for the company

- information about our customers and major partners and our relationships with them

- information about the services and products that they could have access to

- information about cross-company processes and policies

- information about what expertise was available to them across the whole of the company.

In addition some basic requests came through for time-saving tools like an up-to-date telephone directory and maps to our offices world-wide.

The focus groups were held in mid-August 1996. By calling on design and technical skills available in different parts of the company and through the efforts of a virtual team who lobbied the appropriate owners of the needed information, Café VIK was launched 11 weeks later, on November 12th, 1996.

The road show
We decided that the launch of the service warranted more than simply an announcement or brochure landing on people's desks. For one thing, it was important to put the service in context. This was one small step on a much

longer journey that involved significantly changing the way we worked as a company. We chose to go out and meet directly with ICL employees to explain why knowledge management was such a critical part of the new service-led ICL. We planned to introduce them to Café VIK and seek their immediate feedback.

Keeping to the spirit of a Café, we invested in some inexpensive café tables and chairs and some coffee pots. By adding six PCs we then had the material we needed to set up 'Café VIK' in standard conference rooms at ICL sites. We prepared a management briefing that emphasised the link between the management of intellectual capital and the creation of business value. A similar employee briefing emphasised some of the practical benefits of being better at sharing knowledge across the company. These briefings would be given to small groups sitting at the café tables before giving them the opportunity for a hands-on session with the Café VIK service on the PCs.

The Café VIK road show made its way to major ICL sites across Western and Central Europe. Visiting Ireland, the Netherlands, Denmark, Sweden, Finland, France, and Poland as well as the major sites in ICL's home country, the U.K., the road show was extremely well-received by all employees. At a gathering of thirty country managers from some of ICL's more distant locations, an equally positive reaction was generated. The fact that this was an initiative done **for** employees rather than **to** them seemed to be welcomed. Also, the ability to get immediate feedback was very helpful to the Project VIK catalyst team.

On its first anniversary in November 1997, the Café VIK service was being used by approximately 10,000 employees of ICL's 19,000. That number is still on an upward trend as awareness of the service continues to spread across the world.

Sustaining a knowledge-sharing environment

As we have learned more about the processes, technology and people issues related to knowledge-sharing, it has become clear that effective knowledge flows need some dedicated support and facilitation. We would suggest that there are six main roles that will become increasingly common in organisations that have recognised knowledge as a key aspect of competitive advantage. These are:

1) **'Chief Knowledge Officer'** - although this may not be the job title selected by every organisation (the title is used more widely in the U.S. than on this side of the Atlantic), the principle is to identify a member of the senior management team to be accountable for the identification and leveraging of critical knowledge assets.

2) **Information Service Provider** - these are the electronic librarians of Information Age organisations. They organise, catalogue, and maintain the knowledge bases that can be accessed through electronic means. In some organisations they also offer a 'help desk' function to search the electronic library for employees. Café VIK is managed by an Information Services team within ICL - we found that without that dedicated resource, information was soon out-of-date and the value of the service diminished in the eyes of the users.

3) **Webmasters** - these are the individuals who maintain the technical infrastructure on which information and knowledge is shared. Generally responsible for the maintenance of an 'intranet' - which in simplistic terms is the deployment of Internet technology within the boundaries of an organisation. This role may be combined with the information service provider role.

4) **Knowledge sponsors** - individuals responsible for the content and deployment of a specific knowledge asset. For example, a sales director might be the knowledge sponsor for the information shared across an organisation about its customers. Though not a full-time job, this is a critical role in knowledge-based organisations.

5) **Knowledge managers/facilitators** - these are often full-time roles, focused on getting maximum value from one or more knowledge assets. For example, a knowledge facilitator might support a project team, ensuring the team members get the information they need on a just-in-time basis. They also ensure that the relevant knowledge is 'harvested' from the team and fed back into the shared knowledge base.

6) **Knowledge owners** - this is a role that the majority of people in an organisation will hold. It is very important to knowledge sponsors, managers and information service providers. All of the information that we share globally through Café VIK has a clearly identified owner who must commit to keeping that information up-to-date. Now that technology makes information so easily shareable, it is critical that the ownership of shared knowledge be taken seriously as a key responsibility. From our experience, this means that managers need to reinforce the importance of the knowledge owner role by weaving it into role descriptions and reward/recognition processes.

Some lessons learned

The principle of identifying an early, tangible win for customer-facing employees is certainly a step we would recommend. However, we have learned a few lessons along the way.

- Significant time can be wasted debating the difference between information management and knowledge management. We believe that it is helpful to think of knowledge as something that comes from an interaction between people - and to view information as raw material for knowledge. Café VIK is a repository of company information but also a map of where you can find company knowledge. We believe that the value of knowledge in people's heads will always exceed the value of information on a database - and that information services should be primarily directed at connecting the right people more effectively.

- Several parts of the company have set up their local equivalents of Café VIK, linked to Café VIK on the intranet, something we support and encourage as we believe in information being managed at the point of origination. However, they discovered (as we did with Café VIK) that setting up these services is relatively easy. The challenge is to keep the content up-to-date and relevant. We discovered that there are some critical roles and information management processes needed to prevent your electronic library from turning into a knowledge junkyard. Without these roles and processes, the information service is useful only for a few months until its novelty value wears off and the content starts to lose currency.

- As content on shared knowledge bases grows, the challenge of making that content easy to navigate also grows. Individuals with library or information science backgrounds can be very helpful members of the team that develops the organisation's information architecture. The driver needs to be the way in which human beings use or find information rather than the technology tools themselves.

Conclusions

Knowledge management should not be viewed as a new area for specialists - it is a responsibility that everyone in a knowledge-based organisation must share, supported by a number of facilitating roles. ICL's CEO Keith Todd has expressed his personal vision that everyone in ICL should have the same access to knowledge across the company as he does as Chief Executive, in order to harness that capability for our customers. By dedicating some enthusiastic change agents to this issue, we feel we are making some significant progress.

3: Management of know-how in an international City law firm.

Gwenda Sippings, Information Manager, Clifford Chance

Experience and knowledge is vital in the work of successful lawyers, and Clifford Chance has recognised the value of gathering and sharing that knowledge by investing seriously in its information services. As the firm has grown, the importance of designing efficient systems to share access to knowledge lawyers generate, knowledge they need to do their work, and knowledge about the firm has increased. This includes information for and about our colleagues in 24 international offices and their activities. All lawyers have computers on their desks and, in some cases via the various libraries, access to office software and the internet and a variety of licensed commercial services.

Within the firm, responsibility for knowledge management systems is shared by the Information Management, Business Development and Technology Groups, all working closely with the lawyers. A number of high level strategy groups with specific areas of responsibility report in to the Information Strategy Group chaired by the Managing Partner. Although the concept of knowledge management is discussed and practised, it is not often used as a specific term in any of the groups or programmes with which we are involved.

One way in which the firm demonstrates the importance it puts on information and knowledge management is its willingness to nominate partners with particular responsibility for information in the main library and individual practice areas. Not only can they support and promote information office initiatives to other lawyers in the group, but they can act as sounding boards for testing new ideas and also apply pressure to achieve results when necessary.

In London there are nearly 1,000 lawyers working in five major practice areas. These practice areas are arranged in smaller groups to deal with specific areas of law. Some lawyers also work in cross-practice area groups, to apply their knowledge to work such as that involving environmental law which can encompass a variety of needs.

The firm has a number of specialist information offices based in the practice areas, which are managed on a day-to-day basis by people with legal and/or information qualifications. Some are qualified lawyers, who have an excellent understanding of lawyers' research needs and the way they approach problems, and who can identify the unique elements of documents presented for indexing.

They can also analyse information and draft documents to add to the collection. Others are qualified librarians who perform an important role in organising collections, and maintaining awareness of information sources and dealing with enquiries. The main library offers a research and reference service and a resource management service to the whole firm, and gives access to fundamental legal and business information. Professional support lawyers add to the firm's information resources by creating standard form agreements and practice notes and researching and analysing special subjects. All library and information staff support research enquiries from their colleagues in international offices, of which some have sophisticated information services, and others rather more basic collections of material.

Know-how items, those both internally and externally generated, are kept in specialist information offices within the different practice areas, in collections of subject-categorised information, alongside external sources in print or electronic form. Where lawyers cannot access information from their own PC, they visit the information offices or contact them by telephone or e-mail to track down the information they need for their work.

Use of intranets

With the advent of internet technologies, the firm decided to adopt an intranet to disseminate information even more efficiently, and having evaluated the essential security issues, our Technology group recommended and installed a network for us.

The main library and the specialist information offices immediately recognised the benefits of using intranets. Our Technology staff gave a presentation on intranets to library and information staff in June 1997. Less than a year later in London all major practice areas and the main library have their own intranet pages. Plans for local content of intranets in our international offices are being discussed and our Technology group is assessing the most appropriate ways in which to enable these to be implemented so that benefits are firmwide.

Although information officers maintain the records in a Microsoft database, the lawyers will search those records as free text through the intranet, and are presented with simple search screens to guide them to retrieve the information they need. An added bonus is that if their search results present them with an internally generated document, or one available on an authoritative internet site, they can click on the reference and access the document immediately from their own desktops.

Contribution and collection of know-how

The importance of contributing know-how to information systems is one with which lawyers are very familiar. It forms the basis of information from which research is carried out, and consists of internal and external sources. In the past, information office staff have tried a variety of methods of encouraging lawyers to donate information or notes of expertise to their collections, from offering champagne for the best quality donation each month, to scanning their document directories to identify internally generated items of particular general value. The problem is not an unwillingness to donate information, but sometimes a lack of appreciation of the potential value of an item to another person, or sometimes purely lack of time to extract interesting documents from a transaction to draw to the attention of the information officer.

The role of the information office staff in keeping themselves up-to-date with business developments in their practice areas is extremely important in ensuring that all possible information is available to the lawyers.

The donation of information to the corporate memory is further encouraged by discussions with lawyers about the contributions they have made to the information collections. Prior to appraisals, information office staff are invited to identify those lawyers who they know have enhanced the collections for the benefits of colleagues by their donations.

As more internal information is collected and indexed on the know-how systems, the lawyers see the names of their colleagues as authors of documents whose work is worthy of inclusion in the know-how systems who therefore become known authorities on particular areas. The more useful the lawyers find the information they retrieve from the know-how systems, the more they donate items to it themselves.

As far as external information is concerned, the library and information staff regularly evaluate subscriptions to existing commercial products and services and constantly monitor developments of new services, by reading and networking in the usual way. These products consist of legal and business services in printed, online/internet, CD ROM and disc formats. Some electronic products are licensed for all lawyers to use, some only for specific practice areas. We are constantly analysing the desktop information needs of lawyers, and the role of the library and information service staff in tracking information for them. We are also increasingly in discussion with external service providers to explore ways of integrating their information more closely with our own internal sources.

The library and information office intranet pages have been welcomed as an efficient new way to distribute information to lawyers, and are used not only to direct lawyers to internally generated documents such as minutes of meetings and newsletters, and advisory information about people and resources within their own areas but also to indicate external sites of interest and authority on the internet. Links to the firm's own external website (http://www.cliffordchance.com) can give easy access to the firm's overall profile and objectives, as well as providing access to the text of publications and photos of the partners.

The most effective method for collecting know-how and know-who for the systems remains programmes of regular visits when information office staff can talk with the lawyers, and extract knowledge and information such as donations of documents, or flag work for availability later. Contact between the information and legal staff also raises the profile of the information offices within the practice areas, and enables staff to maintain their knowledge of local expertise, which they can use to direct other lawyers firmwide to their experts. Information staff can also monitor the practice interests of their lawyers, and this helps them to tailor information products, such as guides to resources and overviews of the emerging trends in the law. It also helps them with the essential task of promptly alerting the lawyers to changes in the law which will affect their business.

The underlying importance of communication between people within the firm is as true for us as for any other firm. Our vision is to increase the sharing of information and knowledge firmwide and worldwide, and our strategies and technologies are helping us to achieve this.

References and further reading

Aitchison, J, Gilchrist, A & Bawden, D (1997) Thesaurus construction and use: a practical manual. 3rd edition. London: Aslib

Allday, D (1997) Spinning straw from gold: managing intellectual capital effectively. London: Institute of Management

Badaracco, J L (1991) The knowledge link: how firms compete through strategic alliances. Cambridge, Massachusetts: Harvard Business School Press

Badenoch, D, Reid, C, Burton, P, Gibb, F & Oppenheim, C (1994) The value of information *in* Feeney, M & Grieves, M editors.(1994) The value and impact of information. British Library Research Information Policy Issues series. London: Bowker Saur

Basker, J (1998) Intranets: who's doing what. *Business Information Review*, Vol 15 No 2, 94-103

Bonaventura, M (1997) The benefits of a knowledge culture. *Aslib Proceedings*, Vol 49, No 4, April, 82-89

Broadbent, M (1998) The phenomenon of knowledge management: what does it mean to the information profession? *Information Outlook*, Vol 2, No 5, May, 23-36

Chase, R L (1997) The knowledge-based organization: an international survey. *Journal of Knowledge Management*, Vol 1, No 1, September, 38-49

Crawford, J (1996) Evaluation of library and information services. London: Aslib

Eadie, M (1998) Down to earth solutions come out of orbit + Making the most of metals with memory. *Financial Times*, 28 April, 15

Goodger, B (1998) The legal implications of knowledge management. *Knowledge Management*, June, 37

Govindarajan, V & Gupta, A (1998) Turning global presence into global competitive advantage. *Financial Times*, 6 Feb, *Mastering Global Business supplement*, p.46

Hamel, G (1995) The prize that lies in seeing the future. *Financial Times*, 5 June

Hope, T & Hope, J (1997) Chain reaction. *People Management*, 25 Sept, 26-29,31

The IMPACT Programme (1995) Information as an asset: the board agenda. A consultative report. + Checklist and explanatory notes. London: IMPACT PROGRAMME

Journal of Knowledge Management. A quarterly journal, Bedford: IFS International

Ketelhohn, W (1996) Toolboxes are out; thinking is in. *Financial Times, Supplement: Mastering Management Part 20*, 22 March, pp.7-8.

Knowledge Management. A monthly journal, Oxford: Learned Information Europe

Lester, T (1996) Measuring human capital. *Human Resources*, May/June, pp. 54-58

Managing Information. A monthly journal, London: Aslib

Malde, B (1992) What price usability audits? The introduction of electronic mail in a user organization. *Behaviour & Information Technology*, 11 (6), pp345-353

Nicholas, D (1996) Assessing information needs: tools and techniques. London: Aslib

Nonaka, I (1989) Organising innovation as a knowledge-creation process: a suggestive paradigm for self-renewing organization. Working Paper, University of California at Berkeley, No.OBIR-41

Nonaka,I & Takeuchi, H (1995) The knowledge-creating company. Oxford: Oxford University Press

Quelin, B V (1998) Learning more by learning together. *Financial Times*, 13 Feb, *Mastering Global Business supplement*, p.6

Rajan, A, Lank, E & Chapple, K (1998) Good practices in knowledge creation and exchange. Tunbridge Wells: CREATE (the Centre for Research in Employment and Technology in Europe)

Robinson. G & Kleiner, B H (1996) How to measure an organization's intellectual capital. *Managerial Auditing Journal*, Vol 11, No 8, 36-39

Roos, J (1998) How to thrive in the knowledge economy. *Financial Times*, 27 Feb, *Mastering Global Business supplement*, p.14

Rosenzweig, P (1998) Strategies for managing diversity. *Financial Times*, 6 March, *Mastering Global Business supplement*, p.2

Sistla, M & Todd, J (1998) Warning: a killer mistake in business - don't let technology drive your requirements. *Information Outlook*, June, 19-24

Skyrme, D J (1998) Measuring the value of knowledge. London: Business Intelligence

Skyrme, D J & Amidon, D M (1997) Creating the knowledge-based business. London: Business Intelligence

Stonier, T (1990) Information and the internal structure of the universe. London:Springer-Verlag

Sveiby, K A (1997) The new organizational wealth: managing and measuring knowledge-based assets. San Francisco: Berrett-Koehler

Sveiby, K A & Lloyd, T (1987) Managing Knowhow: add value by valuing creativity. London: Bloomsbury

Urquhart, C J & Hepworth, J B (1995) The value of information services to clinicians: a toolkit for measurement. Aberystwyth: Open Learning Unit, DILS, University of Wales

Vernon, M (1998) High scores for the sharing of knowledge. *Financial Times*, 1 April, *IT supplement*, viii.

Ward, V (1998) Overcoming resistance to rough guides at NatWest. *Knowledge Management*, June, 15

Webb, S P (1996) Know-How and information provision in legal firms: individual knowledge and experience as part of the corporate information resource. British Library Research & Innovation Report No.1. Berkhamsted: Sylvia P Webb

Wilson, D A (1996) Managing knowledge. Oxford: Butterworth-Heinemann in association with the Institute of Management

N.B. It is also worth visiting some of the numerous Websites on the subject.

Dr Pauline Berry has complied a list of Web sites of groups working in *knowledge management.* **http://www.dis.strath.ac.uk/people/pb/lots-of-links/KMlinks.html**

The Knowledge Connection, a site put up by David Skyrme Associates, *offers free briefing papers and a monthly update on the subject.* **http://www.skyrme.com**

Appendix: Useful organisations and contacts

(In some cases these are listed without a postal address but welcome contact via their electronic addresses as shown.)

Aslib, The Association for Information Management
Staple Hall, Stone House Court
London EC3A 7PB
Great Britain
Tel: +44 (0) 171 903 0000
Fax: +44 (0) 171 903 0011
email: aslib@aslib.co.uk
http://www.aslib.co.uk/
(Regularly organises seminars, attends conferences and publishes titles on knowledge management. Also provides consultancy services).

Australian Library and Information Association
PO Box E441
Kingston ACT 2604
Australia
email: enquiry@alia.org.au
http://www.alia.org.au

Entovation International
email: debra@entovation.com
http://www.entovation.com

The IMPACT Programme Limited
The International Press Centre
76 Shoe Lane
London EC4A 3JB
Great Britain
email: info@impact-sharing.com
tel: +44 (0)171 842 7900

Knowlege Associates
Knowledge Management Consultants
(Ron Young, Chief Executive)
email: ronyoung@knowledgeassociates.com

Knowledge Research Institute Inc.
5211 Vicksburg Drive
Arlington, TX 76017-4941
USA
email: 7111.1427@compuserve.com

Library & Information Commission
2 Sheraton Street
London W1V 4BH
Great Britain
tel: +44 (0)171 411 0059
email: libcom@lic.bl.uk
http://www.lic.gov.uk
(N.B. This address will shortly change
but is correct at the time of writing.
Updates via the Website.)

David Skyrme Associates
email: david@skyrme.hiway.co.uk
http://www.skyrme.com

Special Libraries Association
1700 Eighteenth Street, NW
Washington DC 20009-2514
USA
Tel: 1-202-234 4700
email: sla@sla.org
http://www.sla.org.membership.irc.eip.html

Dr Karl A Sveiby
http://www.eis.net.au/~karlerik/index.html